Sexy WITH NO BOUNDARIES

What others are saying about Hidi Lee

Hidi Lee offered her audience a beautiful speech. She combined her experience, humor, and insight to our event "Mind, Body, Wellness" at the College of the Canyons University. Coming to the event, our students were very inquisitive about the future "trends" of the fashion industry as well as learning about how to be their own "image consultant." And that's exactly what they got from Ms. Lee's presentation. They took notes on the upcoming fashion trends, including colors, fabrics, and various styles/cuts. Hidi Lee also shared a very personal story of her own mother's initial disapproval of her choice to design "lingerie" within the fashion industry. Many of our students could relate as they listened to her empowering story. This story allowed students to recognize that it is important to find and follow their passion, as well as to never give up on their dreams.

The knowledge she shared was very-well received and appreciated. It is without hesitation that I would recommend Hidi Lee to speak at your event or institution. Her enthusiasm, expertise, and overall viewpoints about beauty, strength, and self-esteem are powerful and enlightening.

—**Tammy L. Mahan**, Psychology Professor,
College of the Canyons

In Hidi Lee's 'To Be Your Own Image Consultant' intensive, I was challenged to find out what my Fashion DNA is to dress myself. And I did just that. Because of that experience, I am able to share with my coaching clients a different angle on self-confidence. It was really amazing how Hidi was able to bring out a couple of details, even the smallest detail that will help you with your everyday dressing. Having an expert like Hidi come in and just turn on the light bulb was life-changing. I am really glad that I spend the day with Hidi and thank you very much, Hidi!

—**Debe Bloom**

I have a fashion business; Hidi's intensive is going to help me work with my customers. The knowledge of color and fashion not only will enhance my products, but will also enhance myself, and my appearance, because I have never been a fashion diva. With the information I received, I am so ready! I have so much more to offer to my customers with my products. Thank you for all the valuable information that you have given to us today.

—**Alicia Harris**

I attended Hidi Lee's intensive. A week later, I was able to have a conversation with my wife regarding fashion. Wow! She was impressed! I didn't think at my age I would be able to have a meaningful conversation with my wife about fashion, I thought it was too late. Not so. My wife was impressed with the knowledge that I now have and how I was able to help her out–in fact I helped her pick out some clothing. I changed my image, and as a result, I was able to bring that home, she actually embraced that. I came out of Hidi's one-day with so much information, that it changed my relationship with my wife and it changed me. Thank you so much, Hidi!

—**Bert Garcia**

The one thing that I valued the most from Hidi's intensive is to make the right decision of what to buy based on a small budget… Because that is the thing very challenging for college students. On top of that, I learned about my body type and my skin tone. For anybody that is in school, and leaning towards the fashion industry, I think they should really take this intensive. It will benefit even those in retail sales or managers to further understand the products they are selling and help clients to choose the piece that works best to them. Thank you Hidi!

—**Monica Generalao**

I found Hidi Lee's coaching valuable. It was fun to talk about fashion with a designer who is currently designing for upcoming seasons and hear what the trends are. It was also good to get confirmation of things, like my body type and what looks good on me. I have a strong fashion sense/background in fashion already, so it was fine-tuning and getting clarity. I think Hidi's coaching would make a big impact with people that don't have any idea how to change/improve their style. Her tips to my fashion challenge were genius. Her support and cheery optimism felt great. I felt heard and understood, really rare in most conversations. Good job!

—**Deirdre Wagner**

At first I thought that Hidi's class was only for women, let me tell you something, as a man, I learn so much-my personality, my skin tone, my body shape; not only that, I learn how to budget my clothes…I am going to look fantastic no matter where I go…at Starbucks, or the Sicilian Sunday Dinner, I am going to be the Fashion Prince. I encourage each one of you to go to her next intensive, Ciao!

—**Maurice DiMino**

I learned so much from Hidi Lee about how to put myself together; how to budget my wardrobe for the future; how to reflect my personality from the inside to the outside. It is a remarkable experience. I think it is a terrific day!

—**Marena Murray**

Hidi did a fantastic job at her intensive! She has a passion for teaching us and it is incredible useful. In my case, I was searching for a personal appearance or brand for my business. I don't want to be over dress or under dress. She gave me some great ideas. She worked with each one of us on what specifically works for our body type, our color. She was fabulous! I highly recommend her to anybody who is interested in retail, or selling themselves, no matter what their products are. Whether you own your own company, or you work for someone else, I recommended reaching out to Hidi, she can change your perspective.

—**Marcia Bruce Bush**

Little that I know, that with all of Hidi's expertise, I now know how to go shopping, a little smarter, a little wiser. Where to find clothes a little less expensive, so that I look the best I can be. I am so happy that I attended Hidi's "To Be Your Own Image Consultant-Discover Your Own Fashion DNA" intensive and I can't wait to tell everyone all about it. Great Job Hidi!

—**Caren Taubman Glasser**

I just attended Hidi's intensive and now I know how to shop, and I know how to create my professional look with a limited budget. I learned so much about myself, I know that I can take control of my own image. Thank you Hidi!

—**Jessie Chang**

WITH NO BOUNDARIES

DISCOVER THE ART OF BEING *Sexy*

—*Mentally, Physically and Professionally*—

Hidi Lee

NEW YORK

$\mathcal{S}exy$ WITH NO BOUNDARIES

Discover the Art of Being Sexy—Mentally, Physically and Professionally

© 2014 Hidi Lee.

Published in New York, New York, by Morgan James Publishing. Morgan James and The Entrepreneurial Publisher are trademarks of Morgan James, LLC. www.MorganJamesPublishing.com

The Morgan James Speakers Group can bring authors to your live event. For more information or to book an event visit The Morgan James Speakers Group at www.TheMorganJamesSpeakersGroup.com.

The purpose of the book is to educate and entertain. The author or publisher does not guarantee that anyone following the techniques, suggestions, tips, idea, or strategies will become successful. The author and publisher shall have neither liability nor responsibility to anyone with respect to any loss or damage caused, or alleged to be caused, directly by the information contained in this book.

FREE eBook edition for your existing eReader with purchase

_____

PRINT NAME ABOVE

For more information, instructions, restrictions, and to register your copy, go to **www.bitlit.ca/readers/register** or use your QR Reader to scan the barcode:

ISBN 978-1-63047-025-8 paperback
ISBN 978-1-63047-026-5 eBook
ISBN 978-1-63047-028-9 hardcover
Library of Congress Control Number: 2013952875

Cover Design by:
Rachel Lopez
www.r2cdesign.com

Back cover photography by:
Michael Mammano

Editing by:
Susie Fabrocini

In an effort to support local communities, raise awareness and funds, Morgan James Publishing donates a percentage of all book sales for the life of each book to Habitat for Humanity Peninsula and Greater Williamsburg.

Get involved today, visit
www.MorganJamesBuilds.com

Habitat
for Humanity®
Peninsula and
Greater Williamsburg
Building Partner

TABLE OF CONTENTS

FOREWORD

Get ready to discover what sexy truly is. You don't need to be what society views as mainstream sexy, what matters is how you feel about yourself. Reading *Sexy with no Boundaries* by Hidi Lee will not only prompt us to re-think the way we perceive ourselves but it can also help minimize the superficial and unhealthy outlook many of us have about personal image.

As an artist who paints, draws and photographs people's expressive faces, I can relate to the mind set and message Hidi shares with her audience. Hidi has included stories rich with experiences that allow her to identify with how people feel about themselves through all aspects of sexy. Through artistic visuals and self-esteem based triggers we often utilize the fashion that we wear to express ourselves.

In the mind set of *Sexy with no Boundaries* you can strengthen your positive self-image but more importantly embrace your self-worth, your sexy personality and how you take care of yourself. As a self-proclaimed work in progress I rely on art and image to creatively reinvent myself and I support Hidi's message that "sexy is in the eye of the beholder."

Hidi provides several ways to express yourself all throughout her book. I would have greatly benefited to have her book as a pre-teen who often felt awkward and unattractive. Many times the attention I received was for being overweight, for not knowing how to style my hair, wear my makeup or for wearing discount clothing while attending school with kids who dressed like super models. But most unattractive of all was the perception and image of my home life growing up in a house of domestic violence.

As I reached my early twenties, I found my mother's teachings of personal image and self-confidence are as much a state of mind as they are a physical embodiment or set of actions.

I started teaching my mom's philosophies at a local Battered Women's shelter to support women who have suffered similar physical and mental abuse. My mom gave me the strength to believe in myself which coincidently appears in many of the positive examples taught in Hidi's creative book. I will proudly request a signed copy of Sexy with no Boundaries to give to my mom.

Hidi's book embodies messages of feeling and being sexy on so many different levels she is truly an inspiration to others to embrace their inner and outer beauty. She teaches how we are all sexy in our own beautiful way and how it's okay to evolve and experiment with non-traditional ways of expression. She combines an "old school sexy" with a "sexy in the millennium" attitude which is both fun and refreshing.

I actually laughed out loud when I read chapter two "Sexy is the Fugitive from the Red Carpet!" With all of the near wardrobe disasters I've had to avoid while working red carpets as a media correspondent I will now take Hidi's mind set with me each time and "work" the safety pin holding up my sponsored gown with pride. There are several ways to interpret Hidi's message to relate to our own challenges in life. For me the humorous lessons stand out the most since they are fun to share with others.

"Sexy is a Time Capsule" in my own career lingo is one of my favorite "sound bites". As a celebrity image expert, working on live television, in an image competitive world, I too, am faced with the overwhelming expectation of having a time limit for a successful career.

I choose to live by many of Hidi's time capsule principals and embrace a positive and joyous attitude. I've always told myself that it's not about pretty it's about presentation, and now I have multiple chapters of "Sexy with no Boundaries" to back up my personal and professional beliefs. Thank you, Hidi, for writing this book for both men and women of all ages, colors, shapes and sizes. You and your message ARE sexy with no boundaries!

Hidi has out done herself by offering in this book the valuable views, showing all the different aspects of what "being sexy" truly means. "Unveil the imperfection in sexiness" is just one of many messages that show, that it is not your everyday book about how to become a super model to be sexy. This book is also unique in sharing stories and feelings from celebrities as well as those with star style and charisma. I recommend reading *Sexy with no Boundaries* and to embrace the art of being sexy!

Starley Murray

Celebrity Image Expert

"Image is more than what you wear; Image is how you represent yourself in life"

I am very honored to have written this foreword for Hidi Lee's *Sexy with no Boundaries!*

ACKNOWLEDGMENT

Thank you to all the contributors: Adryenn Ashley, Amy Cheryl, Amy Regenstreif, Ardiana Bani Cohn, Brain Kelly, Carol Ann Wagner, Carrie Stewart, Cinthia Gambino-Calderon, Dina Bias, Elle Sompres, Helen Woo, Hind Aleryani, Jack Zufelt, Janet Ogata, Jennifer Bagley, Nicole, Kathlee DePuydt, Maurice DiMino, Mayra Abruzzo Garza, Nancy Ferrari, Nobuko Sezaki, Patricia Gorski, Gagic, Regiane Rhonda Clure, Ricky Powell, Sarah Khan, Sheryl Robinson Bagalio, Siouxsie, Suzy Manning & Svetlana Ray

The birth of *Sexy with no Boundaries* was supported by the many visionaries who've had faith in me and believed in my mission. Their help with bringing this book to reality is very much appreciated.

Thank you to the contributors who shared their true experiences of sexiness—emotionally, physically, mentally, spiritually and professionally. The contributors to this book include (in alphabetic order):

This book would not be as inspiring without the joint efforts of these heartfelt contributors.

I would also like to thank those who bought my first book "Almost Naked-Lingerie, Secret of the Guilty Pleasure". Thank you for supporting me on my journey to discover my mission-A mission to encourage positive self-image.

Thank you to all those who attended my "The Naked Truth" workshop and "To Be Your Own Image Consultant" Intensive. Thank you for allowing me to share my experiences and to empower both men and women to look good and feel sexy both inside and out.

I would like to thank you to the creative team of Morgan James Publisher, including Terry Whalin, David Hancock, Jim Howard, Margo Toulouse, Bethany Marshall and especially Scott Frishman, who believes in me, encourage me and guide me along the way to the birth of this book, the first one of a series.

Thank you to all my family and close friends who have always been my cheerleaders no matter where I am and what I do.

Thank you to my love, my mentor, Maurice DiMino, who brainstormed with me on the concept of this book and the whole series. Your guidance and support is the core of my success. Thank you also to my two handsome young gentlemen, Valerio Lucidi and Alessio Lucidi, who are always proud of me and patient with me. I am so grateful to have you two in my life!

A special thanks to Starley Murray to write my Foreword; Rick Chandler, Mary Cimiluca and Amanda T. to write my reviews and Susie Fabrocini to edit my book.

From the bottom of my heart, thank you all!

Hidi Lee

INTRODUCTION

I don't remember exactly when people stopped calling me "Hidi". Instead, it was replaced by "Sexy". "Hi Sexy!" "Sexy Mamma!" I always thought that people misused the word "sexy". "I am not sexy! I am stylish!" I thought to myself, but I am not going to argue with them.

Until one day while I was talking on the phone with the husband of my best friend, Willy. He said, "My cousin thinks that you are hot and sexy." There, I had to argue with him. I said, "I am not sexy! I am stylish!" Willy insisted, "You are sexy!" "Where am I sexy? I have no boobs!" I protested. "Who told you that sexy has to do with only boobs? You are sexy because of your unique personality, you are sexy because of the way you put yourself together…bahbahbah" he argued. I could not hear one word anymore. I was so confused.

Yes, I was raised in an era, a demographic and a culture that the *"old school sexy"* image was implanted in my head. All along, I thought that sexy had to do with having a nice cleavage; very curvy body, or a very provocative outfit…and I have none of that!

Ladies and Gentlemen, what is sexy to you? Whatever you have in your mind, hold that image! Perhaps your perception of "What is sexy?" is going to change after you finish reading this book.

"Sexy" is a unique English adjective. You can't find a word with the exact same meaning in any other language. There is absolutely no equivalent word. According to the dictionary, it is an adjective—It is *"sexually interesting or exciting; radiating sexuality"*. According to the encyclopedia, Sexy is an adjective that describes sexual attraction in humans, and other species.

So these *"sexually interesting, or radiating sexuality"* or *"sexual attraction"* all seem to be a visual format to me. I decided to spend more time on digging the DNA of sexiness. I looked up to those sexy divas to find out what is sexy to them. To my surprise, both Angelina Jolie and Heidi Klum agreed that scars are sexy. So it tells me that the sexual attraction doesn't have to have a nice cleavage or curvy body figure, or even a provocative outfit. It doesn't have to be perfect at all! In fact, it is the imperfection makes it attractive and arousing sexual interest.

Someone asked me, "Can a voice arouse sexual interest?" Sure! Listen to Rod Stewart's famous song, "Do you think I am sexy?" Whether you think Rod Stewart is physically sexy or not, I am sure his voice is sexy to you. How about Elvis Presley? His voice had attracted millions of women in the world.

Not only did I realized that sexy can be experienced visually or audibly, I found out that it exceeds those boundaries too! When Paris Hilton said that she found self confidence to be sexy, it made me think of Willy's comment about me being sexy with my unique personality. Sexy does has a very diverse dimension!

I started to realize there is an *"old school sexy"* where visual format dominates. The older generation was flooded with the pin-up, sexy, flirty, curvy women's bodies. In the past, there wasn't much celebration of men's bodies. Nor did they talk about sexiness beyond the visual aspect. Today there is a shift in focus. We appreciate male figures as well as female, and we are aware that sexuality is expressed and experienced in many ways beyond the visual.

Yes, sexy is being redefined! The whole meaning of sexy has been up-graded to a more intelligent and sophisticated level where people celebrate the internal beauty, whether it is the mental, emotional or spiritual aspect. This is *"sexy in the millennium"*. These criteria weren't set in the dictionary, or encyclopedia. They didn't exist in the old days. In fact, when a society changes, certain established concepts change to reflect the latest life style, mentality and commodity. So these days, *"sexy"* is a more profound and deeper experience. I think the "old school sexy' and the "sexy in the millennium" must be combined. The visual attractiveness, combined with the more important aspects of attitude, personality and self maintenance.

Of course, "old school sexy" is the first impression. With a good first impression, people want to know more; to know who you are inside because you drew their attention and now they are hooked. And once they look beyond the external beauty, the inner beauty will take control. I still remember when I watched the movie "Snow White", both Snow White and the witch are beautiful. But Snow White is beautiful inside and out, while the witch is only beautiful on the outside. She is ugly on the inside. That's why she is a witch! Although it is a fairy tale, the concept never change, no matter what era, what geographic territories is, inner beauty will always beat out external beauty in the long run.

I have lived and worked in seven cities, four countries and three continents. Currently, I live in Los Angeles, home of countless celebrities, actors, actresses...the flawlessly beautiful icons-that we try to model. Mass media tells us what is sexy and we buy their products to try to conform, often creating undue stress as we try to attain the unattainable. As we admire the perfect faces and perfect figures, we suffer from the haunting disappointment of not having those features ourselves. Those who suffer the most are the teenagers who are still molding their values, their attitudes, their personalities. They are especially sensitive to the demands of peer pressure.

I've also witnessed countless mature individuals who are confused and insecure, lacking confidence in themselves. Whether they are over-weight, under-weight, divorced, single moms, cancer survivors, victims of child abuse / sex abuse…all suffer from serious self esteem issues, because they think that they cannot measure up to the public's expectations. That is exactly my motivation for writing this book.

There is no solid definition for what is sexy; it varies from one to another. Sexy has no boundaries! Sexy is beauty-blind, sexy is color-blind, sexy is size-blind, sexy is age-blind, sexy is gender-blind, sexy is cultural-blind and sexy is religion-blind! Sexy is in the eye of the beholder! Sexy is within everybody-you, me, men, women-even an object, a product can be sexy. How many of you have come across a streamlined luxury car and thought, "How sexy is that car!"

Sexy is within yourself. You don't need to be perfect. It's in the corners of your eyes, it's in the tips of your smile, it's in the scar on your cheek, it's in the wrinkles around your eyes. It is the unique personality that you carry with you. It is the energy that you radiate. It is the confidence that you show in the way you talk. Sexy has no boundaries. We are all sexy in our own way!

"Sexy with no Boundaries" is a compilation of real life stories from contributors from all across the world. They represent different genders, different ages, different religions, different cultures, different sizes, different ethnicities and different professions. Aiming to explore the profound meaning of what the individual experiences as "sexy", this book will awaken the depths of the soul and the mind-beyond the social boundaries. I believe that we have to re-educate society to break through false body perceptions. Together, we are going to make a better world!

"Do I consider myself sexy?
It all depends on the way I'm feeling.
When I'm happy inside,
that's when I feel most sexy."
~ Anna Kournikova

"A great figure or physique is nice,
but it's self-confidence
that makes someone really sexy."
~ Vivica Fox

"Sexy at the millennium means
having a solid sense of self
but never taking yourself
too seriously."
~Rebecca Romijn Stamos

Chaper 1

"Being strong can be also feminine.
I don't think feminine equals being weak.
Being strong is very sexy."
~ Sanaa Lathan

"A well-developed sense of humor
is the pole that adds balance to your steps
as you walk the tightrope of life."
~ William Arthur Ward

"How tall am I? Honey, with hair,
heels and attitude
I'm through this damned roof."
~ Drag Queen RuPaul

"For beautiful eyes, look for the good in others;
for beautiful lips, speak only words of kindness;
and for poise, walk with the knowledge that you are never alone."
~ Audrey Hepburn

There are five elements that contribute most to the *"SEXY DNA"*. They are "Mind Set", "Happiness", "Sense of Humor", "Self Love" and "Confidence". They are different from each other but they are contagious towards each other.

Mind Set

Few years ago I was going through a very difficult marriage and I was very unhappy. The failure of my marriage was wearing me down. I could see that I changed into a different person. I no longer had a positive vision in life. I could feel the negative emotions that ran through my blood, into my veins and into my throat. I came so close to throwing up because of the taste of sourness and bitterness within my soul. I realized that I had to do something to stop this evil emotion from poisoning me.

Of course, I am a professional lingerie designer and I dress my part. People always call me "sexy." I might have looked sexy, but emotionally, I didn't feel sexy inside. Not only that, I felt I lost my femininity. The fact that I was the bread-winner of the family made me actually feel like a man. I might look like a sexy woman, but deep inside, I felt like a heartless man with almost no sensitivity. What is femininity? I was lost.

After I got divorced, my emotion became more calm and peaceful. I became happier. Even though I did not have a boyfriend, I was happy to get out from an unsuccessful relationship. I was ready to start a new chapter of my life and I was ready to be happy again. I told myself whether I found someone or not, it doesn't define my happiness. I am happy to be my true self. I am blessed to have two very wonderful sons. I am blessed to be healthy-mentally, emotionally, physically and financially. I am blessed to find peace within myself.

While my children got older, I started to spend some time improving myself. My circle of friends grew bigger since I joined Toastmasters, a place where we learn to be better communicators. Then one day I went to a Toastmasters Christmas party where there was a woman who performed a Hula Dance. It was the first time I saw a live Hula Dance. I knew the performer; I had known her for a few months then. To me, she was an average looking woman. I swear that I had never related her with the word "sexy" until I saw her dance. Every single move of hers-her hip and her hands were so well coordinated, she was filled with confidence, and gracefulness and she screamed femininity to me. It was definitely a jaw-dropping experience for me. A strange feeling ran through my veins and I felt her sexiness. After that, I fell in love with Hula Dancing. It was a very feminine, very graceful and a very sexy dance.

I decided to learn Hula Dance. Soon I found myself dancing in front of the mirror of the dancing studio. I watched my own hands and body moving gracefully along the romantic music. I felt that I was finally a woman again. I finally saw the sexy side of me deep from the most vulnerable part of my anatomy. More importantly, it was in my mind again.

I am forever grateful for my decision to learn Hula. That was an important step for me in finding not only my passion and sensuality, but it also improved my posture, confidence, and self-esteem. You see, it is actually a "chicken and egg" theory. It is the sexiness that makes you feel confident; but it is also the confidence that makes you sexy!

You can think of something that makes you feel sexy or think of something that gives you confidence. I highly recommend that you start to do things that turn you on! You are going to own it once you feel it inside of you. In The Emerald Tablet-"As above, so below; as within, so without", it shows that whatever holds true in heaven, will be the same on earth. Whatever resides on the inside should come out to play on the outside. Set your positive mind and see how your mood or confidence changes along.

In Joel Osteen's book "Every Day a Friday", he talks about a blind senior citizen looking for a new place after his wife went to be with the

Lord. This gentleman hired a real estate agent. When she took him to visit the potential senior citizen home, he said, "I like it" as she was describing how the front yard and the foyer looked. He kept saying, "I like it! I like it! I like it!" She said, "Wait until I tell you how the living room and the kitchen is." He said, "Whether I like it or not doesn't depend on how the furniture is arranged, I have already programmed in my head that I am going to like this place."

He set in his mind that he is going to like the place, and he did. Some call it "stubborn", I call it "determined". Same as everything in life, when you set your mind to be happy; you will be happy. When you set your mind to be brave; you are going to be brave. When you set yourself to be sexy; you will be sexy! It is a mind set. It is an attitude! It starts at the inner most of you.

Happiness

Iris Apfel, the fashion icon, once said, *"All the plastic surgery in the world isn't going to help if you are unhappy."* So true, a happy average looking person is far more attractive than an unhappy beauty queen. Happiness is inviting, it is up-lifting. A simple smile can melt someone's heart. A genuine smile can steal someone's soul. It breaks the boundaries of different cultures, different languages, and different geographic territories. Who doesn't want to be surrounded by happy people? Happiness is contagious! I remember I saw a YouTube Video of a person who started laughing inside a metro train. First; the other people around him looked at him wondering why the man was laughing so hard. Then, after a while, one after another, everyone inside the metro train began to laugh without even knowing why. Yes, happiness is contagious! Whatever laugh it might be—giggling, cackling, laughing out loud, laughing to tears, gentle laughing, friendly smiling or smiling from the heart, they are all priceless and free! You just can't put a dollar sign on it. And they all bring joy to your heart!

People from all over the world seek for happiness. Whether you are helping people because it makes you happy, or you play a joke on your friend, or you finish a project on time, or you got what you were dreaming for…so many possibilities, but only one result-happiness!

Dalai Lama mixes his spiritual and philosophical wisdom into his book "The Art of Happiness". He shares how people should look beyond the external events, and find happiness based on compassion, kindness, and the fundamental goodness in all human beings. That is true and lasting happiness.

Contentment is a very subtle kind of happiness. I will never forget what I learned from the TV program "Kung Fu" when I was a child. The little monk had this conversation with his Master Kung Fu Monk. The little monk complained, "I feel lonely." "Close your eyes!" commanded the Master Monk. The little monk did just that. Master Monk asked, "What do you hear now?" The little monk listened intensely for a little while, and then he said, "I hear the birds sing, the sound of the blowing wind, and the sound of the running river." "You see? You are not lonely! When you have a clear mind, you will realize that you are not alone. Be content with things around you. Pay attention and appreciate every little thing around you. You will learn the master of happiness-the inner peace!"

Instead of chasing after superficial happiness, you should not only love those who are supportive of you, but also practice patience and tolerance towards your detractors. Compassion will follow and that is the essence of a spiritual life.

Sense of Humor
In the book "The Phantom Tollbooth", written by Norton Juster, the Sense Taker can steal your sense of purpose, take your sense of duty, or destroy your sense of proportion, but he can never take your sense of humor. With that, you have nothing to fear. Indeed, a sense of humor

is powerful and influential. It is one of the greatest assets a person can have. Even though "sense of humor" is ranked highly for both men and women when asked about the important attributes of their partners; their expectations for each other are different. While women are attracted by men who make them laugh; men, on the other hand, are looking for women who laugh at their jokes. As such, men are the "generators" while women are the "appreciators".

Humor is a part of a big family that includes laughter, amusement and smiling. Having a sense of humor means being able to see the humor in life's imperfections—whether it is a "Laugh out loud" or "put a smile on your face" type of humor. Laughter is the greatest reward of being alive. You don't need to be funny to have a sense of humor. Of course, if you are funny, it is really a gift. This quality is charming to both sexes. After all, who doesn't want to be entertained by people who are funny?

It is not necessary for you to be funny, but being able to appreciate another's sense of humor will add to your personal charm. The individual perception of humor often depends on one's geographical location, cultural background, religious heritage, maturity, educational level, intelligence and context.

Jennifer Jones once said, *"If you could choose one characteristic that would get you through life, choose a sense of humor.* That sounded odd when I first read it, but upon further examination, I can see why a sense of humor is so important. It is not just about having fun, or laughing; but it's the ability to see the lighter side of anything. That can help you to ease your stress; get through challenging times in life; diffuse difficult situations; guide your tough decisions, ease your mental pressure and heal your wounded soul. It is the transformation from the "HALF EMPTY glass of water" to "HALF FULL glass of water". After all, you only live once, why not chose the positive one?

That is why it is so important to have a sense of humor.

Most women admit that they are attracted to men who have a sense of humor. They consider it to be far more important than having attractive features or a good body. Why is this so? We are attracted by people who have a big heart. The ability to be silly or to be able to laugh at your own mistakes is an art-an art that helps people rebound from an awkward situation.

Most men feel connected when they discover that their partner shares their sense of humor. They feel compatible when their partners burst out laughing at their jokes. They feel that their inner quality is being recognized and appreciated, and they experience an increased self confidence. Whether you tell funny jokes or appreciate and laugh at funny jokes, if you can find joy in every aspect of your life, you will have good life. Looking for a reason to laugh wherever you are, whatever you do, whoever you are with, can help you brighten the day, in good times, or in bad.

Having a good sense of humor makes you happier and healthier. It enhances the immune system, makes it easier to withstand pain, and lengthens the life span! And it doesn't matter if you are rich, or poor; young, or old; or what your skin color is, life is good when you can laugh frequently!

**There are 4 major ways to improve,
or enhance your sense of humor**

1. Treasure the simple pleasures: I remember many times when I was on my way home after a whole day of working in my office; I could not stop smiling from the depths of my heart. I could not get home fast enough to cook for my sons. The joy of knowing that I have someone that I love to pamper and take care of caused the sweetest smile to appear on my face. I can't even tell you how very blessed I felt to have my two wonderful sons. I really enjoy cooking for them. I felt blessed. This is a simple

pleasure! Remember to acknowledge such simple pleasures, because they are priceless!

2. Reward yourself with the gift of laughter-whether it is a comedy show, a silly movie, or a light book, it lifts your mood and brightens your day. My Toastmasters club has a role as "Joke Master" in between the voting sections. Instead of having people get up and running around the room, or chatting amongst themselves, we created this role so that it gives the members another opportunity to speak in front of the crowd. I found that this role is very fruitful. Not only does the Joke Master have the chance to share his/her jokes, but it also bonds the members together. It creates a light and friendly atmosphere in the serious setting.

3. Don't be shy to share with others your silly or embarrassing experiences. Focus humor on yourself. By revealing your vulnerable moments, it shortens the distance between you and your audience. After all, being able to laugh at yourself is an art.

4. Learn how to turn a sour mood or a dark moment into something light and silly. Find a way to laugh when something annoys or frustrated you. It is not easy, but if you can master it, it is one of the most precious life lessons. I remember when I told my boyfriend how tough my up-bringing was. Instead of feeling sad along with me, he said, "And look how great you've become, congratulations!" Indeed, you can feel sorry and hold onto the things that happened in the past; or you can see how you overcame the difficulty and pulled yourself up! Life is too short to be grumpy. Dalai Lama also believes facing our enemy is the best opportunity to practice compassion, so our enemy is a great teacher.

Try to practice these four ways on a daily basis, you will see that not only will you be happier, but you will also be a bigger person in life!

Self Love

You are a Millionaire! No, I am not kidding you! Let me explain this to you.

I attended "Night of Hope" by Joel Osteen at the Staples Center in Los Angeles in October 2012. During his sermon, he talked about an article that he read from a Medical Magazine. It published research from a group of scientists who did a calculation on how much an average human body is worth. It includes the cost of the cells, organs and tissues, etc. The result concluded that a person with an average size body is worth about 6 million dollars! Joel added, "It is ONLY for the average size person; if you are bigger, you could worth 9 million Dollars! You see? You are not over weight; you are just *more valuable!*" He has a good sense of humor!

Before you get so excited, I have even more good news to share with you. We are worth more than our physical property; every one of us owns the most valuable real estate in the world. It is our intellectual property!

According to the World Bank, every person in the US has access to $734,000 worth of intellectual assets! Have you heard of "A Million Dollar idea"? When you realize the worth of your knowledge and wisdom, idea or invention, recipe or formula…you will know that you own a hidden treasure, just waiting to be cashed out!

Now, I know that in your head, you are calculating how much are you physically and intellectually worth? Six million? Or 9 Million? Plus the Intellectual property, adding $734,000, for those who are bigger than the average size, you might be worth close to 10 million dollars!

Human beings have a common behavior. We tend to love something more when we realize that it is valuable. So now that you know how valuable you are, do you think that you love yourself more?

I love antiques and especially glass sculptures. A while ago, I went to an antique shop and I saw a beautiful glass figurine. Not only was it signed by the artist, but also marked as "limited edition"! I fell in love with it and after some bargaining; I got it for only $60 dollars. I brought it home and did some research on the internet. I found two websites that sell this same piece. One asked for $490, and the other one asked for $800! I was so excited! I knew that I made a good purchase! I knew that I loved this piece the first time I laid my eyes on it, but now I love it even more!

Numbers are magical, but don't let them fool you. Never judge whether you are attractive or successful by the number in your age; the numbers on your scale; the number in your dress; and the number you have in your bank account. They are just numbers and your value has nothing to do with them.

That explains why so often, we see very famous individuals commit suicide at the peak of their career. You might think that they have everything-fame, fortune, soul mate and beautiful bodies…that pretty much accounts for everything you could want in life, right? But they lack the most important thing in their lives. It is their self value-how worthy they believe themselves to be. Some think that just because their partner left them for another, it means that they are not worthy anymore. Some think that they are not pretty enough to be successful in anything. Some think that because they were laid-off from their job; or went bankrupt in their business; or lost their house to foreclosure, they consider themselves as "failures". They don't feel worthy anymore.

Your value is how much you think you are worth. Just like a piece of art, its value depends on how much the buyer is willing to pay. How much are you willing to pay for yourself? Priceless! Right?

Understand that nobody is perfect, so why should you be? Just like Bob Proctor, the Philosopher in "The Secret", he literally kissed himself (he kissed his own arms and hands)! Tell yourself how beautiful and intelligent you are. Fall in love with every single part of your body. Love yourself unconditionally because you are worth millions!

Confidence

Remember what I said before? The major ingredients in the *"SEXY DNA"* are "Mind Set", "Happiness", "Sense of Humor", "Self Love" and "Confidence". They are different from each other but they are related to each other. I believe that the common ground for all of them is buried inside us.

I think the best way to be sexy is working from the inside out. As Jim Kwik said, *"If an egg is broken by outside force, LIFE ends. If broken by inside force, LIFE begins. Great things always begin from inside."* If you just have the look, but do not have the inner mind set, you are not putting the two together. The sexiness is not complete. If you are comfortable in your own skin, you are most likely a confident person. In my research about being sexy, I found out that confidence contributes most of the sexiness. If you have a positive attitude in life, you are most likely a person that can see the positive in any negative situation. If you have faith in life, you are most likely a peaceful person. If you have a sense of humor, you are most likely a fun and happy person who can keep things in perspective.

If you are a driven, self-motivated person, you are most likely a leader. If you are kind and sympathetic, you are most likely surrounded with faithful friends. If you take good care of your body and if you are aware of the food that you eat, you are most likely a healthy person. If you take responsibility financially, you are most likely a self-sufficient person. If you are creative, you are most likely an interesting person. If you are disciplined, you will most likely enjoy your relationship with your partner. If you are passionate about what you do, you are more likely to become a successful person, because you can only excel when you love what you do.

In the book, "The Secret", it states, "You become who you think you are." Human minds are the most powerful tool in the whole universe. We create our reality from how we set our mind. What you feel internally will project outward and attract that same energy that you set inside of you. This is the Law of Attraction!

We are all attracted by confident people, so it makes sense that we become the person we are attracted to. Think of what kind of a person that you are attracted to. Then it makes sense if you carry that kind of quality in you, because the same elements always attract each other. So if you appreciate great inner qualities such as authenticity, optimism, sense of humor, confidence, great attitude and driven personality, work within yourself to get those qualities. Then you will find yourself surround by people who have those same qualities as you. Sexy is a by-product of all these fabulous inner qualities.

Happiness is Sexy!
By Ricky Powell

Happiness is Sexy!

Since I am known as, "The Happiness Guy," you can probably guess my answer to the question, "What do you think is sexy?" For me, it is a truly happy woman.

In fact, when I see a woman who is self confident, smiling and projecting a bright, positive image, I would say she goes far beyond the idea of sexy and steps right into stunning.

There is something very special about a lady who has mastered the art of Lifelong Happiness and is living day to day by all the tenants that make up a happy and meaningful life. Someone who lives with gratitude deep down in her soul and is grateful for all that she has in her life, not just the big things but the little things as well.

Someone who loves helping others, not for what she can gain but what she can give to enrich their lives and help them achieve their biggest goals and dreams.

Sexy is a woman who knows how to take care of herself by getting just the right amount of sleep, nutrition and exercise so that she not only looks her best but also feels like she is on top of the world.

Forgiveness is something she would know well. Harboring anger does nothing except punish the person holding onto that anger, so knowing this, she would want nothing to do with holding onto any of those negative emotions like hate, anger, jealousy, resentment, entitlement or anything of that nature.

Additionally, she would value people and relationships over material possessions and status. Human relationships are the foundation for living a rich, meaningful life. Seeking out positive, like-minded people is a great way to begin building these associations.

There would be no need for complaining, criticizing or gossiping, ever.

Having been in the happiness business for several years now, I've had the wonderful opportunity to meet so many people who enjoy creating and experiencing a positive mindset, which is where the seeds of happiness begin.

For me, someone who is best known for being, "The Happiness Gal" would be very sexy indeed!

Being Sexy
By Cinthia Gambino-Calderon

Oh, what IS sexy? Who defines this anyway? Who sits back and judges who is to be considered sexy and who is not? I guess I never really wondered that until I thought of writing this. That is when I realized that each one of us decides who and what is sexy, and how and when we feel sexy.

This realization prompted me to look back at my life. Thinking and judging myself about being sexy depending on the outfit I was wearing. I remember that in my 20's I would go to the clubs and felt sexy. However, there was one night I went to a club in a different city and a girl approached me in the ladies room and modified my outfit to make it sexier. That meant that the style I had worn before was not considered sexy in this place and this girl just took mercy on me. This club required that skin was bare to be considered sexy.

Later in my 30's I discovered my own sexy. This is something I believe happens very often with women in our 30's. I became aware that the sexiness that I possessed was not coming from the outfits I wore. I felt great in my skin. I became aware that being healthy and fit gave me confidence that no amount of make up or skimpy outfit could ever give me. Then I also started noticing it in other people. There is something sexy about the underlined confidence that is present when a person knows, loves, and nurtures their own being.

Some may say that confidence comes to a person when they are handsome or beautiful, but that is not the case at all. There have been plenty of people who have come in and out of your life; as well as mine, that I am sure you can think of right now who have the looks but nothing to back it up with. And even as I mention it, it's easy to think of who I am talking about, right? Ok, that is not for me to judge, but I do have my opinions about people who choose not to think for themselves, and maybe I'll get the opportunity to write about that in another contribution. This time however, let's focus on the sexy path that took me on the road to finally getting my sexy back.

My desire to become a well rounded person made me look at where my life was out of balance. I felt internally confident, but mentally, I felt I needed to accomplish something more. I decided that in order to gain some balance I needed to see what earning a master's degree would provide. I was curious about business and my goal became to earn a graduate degree. At this point I had been working with a group of women and teenage girls that encouraged sisterhood, and I was bitten by the bug of forming a non-profit organization to serve our younger generation of sisters. By the end of earning my graduate degree I felt confident in being sexy, and being smart, but I also realized that forming a non-profit organization was an uphill battle. At the end when I turned in my last paper for school I went on a 6 or 8 mile run. I don't remember exactly, I just remember being hyped up about finally being done, and I ran, and ran, and ran. I felt amazing, until the next day.

Physically, I had reached rock bottom for my frame. I was overweight, I felt exhausted, and I would get winded walking up the stairs. I couldn't believe that I was 36 years old and felt like I must be in my late 60's. I decided that for my birthday I wanted a personal trainer. April 2012 marked the beginning of my next personal journey to becoming my kind of sexy. I began to train more seriously and had a goal in mind to become a fitness competitor. I didn't want to do it as a profession, I just wanted to step on stage and be amongst these women who worked so hard at looking amazing. Through many changes and challenges, the journey to becoming fit became overwhelming. My life revolved around days and nights of working out and daily meal plans. That means I was constantly thinking about working out or eating. The journey was exhausting and even more difficult than earning a master's degree.

The culmination of the journey ended in the fabulous last three days before the competition. During these days of depletion and preparation I took time off from my full time job. My nails were done, my hair was beautiful and smooth, my eyelashes were curled, the sparkling jewelry was laid out, and the tiniest bikini I had ever owned was all ready to go. The bright red color of the bikini and the rhinestones that lined the straps of the bathing suit marked the passion I had put into this journey. I had given it my all. I thought that no matter what would happen on that day of being on stage didn't matter-well, almost!

The day was here, it was April 13, 2013, the day after my 38th birthday. It had been a long 12 month journey that would end that night. Being surrounded by women who were professionals, was intimidating to those of us who were amateurs, until we all met backstage. The tanned naked bodies could only persuade you to become friendly with one another, after all we were all women on the same depleted diets right? Well, the long hours leading to the final judgment allowed us to get to know each other's journeys. There were women who had overcome cancer and decided that living healthy was their new life and this was why they were doing this. There were some women who were doing this on a dare. There were some women who wanted to test their endurance. Then there were some women like me, who wanted to know what was possible when you put your mind to anything, trust in God, and have your husband's and children's full support.

That afternoon I walked on stage as a competitor, but that night I walked away a winner. I came home with a trophy and a proud 5th place honor. I was amongst the sexiest fit women according to the judges, but in my mind, and in my life, I had reached this dream, and that, well, that is just sexy!

Did someone say "sexy"?

By Carrie Cray-Stewart

"SEXY?" What defines the word "SEXY?"

Some may think the definition would be a Sports Illustrated Model posing half nude on the beach. In my eyes, it's quite the opposite. Beauty and sexiness come from within. I feel it's the entire package with so many hidden qualities composed from the innermost layers of oneself.

Let me begin by expressing what I find to be the real beauty of sexy: A great sense of humor, wittiness, a personality which allows a woman to laugh genuinely, to smile with the utmost appreciation, and the intense excitement of great intimate conversation.

Intelligence is extremely sexy. Just being with someone who can converse on any given topic, and additionally bring some humor to the discussion is sexy.

Okay, I'm going to be honest, the eyes, yes, the eyes can say so much! Now, that's sexy!

If you combine all the qualities I've listed above, that just about sums up the real "SEXY" for me!

Here's one of my little experiences which is proof enough to me that everything I stated above to be true.

Over a year ago, I received an invitation to be a guest on a radio show. The host had included a very lengthy email. I've done many radio interviews in the past, but there was something intriguing about this host. Here I am, a best-selling romance novelist, infatuated by the sexiness of a total stranger! I was completely captivated by the invitation.

To be honest, it was never my intention to slip into the world of this radio personality. He had me from "hello!" I further investigated this radio host, and YES, he was the real thing. His personality, wittiness, humor, and intelligence all added up to my definition of sexy.

One of the sexiest things any man can do to a woman would be to crawl inside her mind and make her imagination run wild…again, 'sexy' is not about the looks, but what comes from deep within.

Love yourself

By Ardiana Bani Cohn

As I was growing up I began to realize that being the center of attention is not always good. I started to feel timid and always cautious about how I looked. Was I pleasant enough, was I nice enough? In fact, I was struggling with which way to go: nice or sexy? When I felt sexy, I attracted many male friends but not so many females. They hated me. When I felt smart and nice, I attracted many female but no male friends.

One day I said "the heck with this, I am going to be myself, whoever likes me as myself, is my true friend." That moment was magical. I attracted male and female friends and I wasn't seen as a pleasure object but as a desirable companion.

What happened then? The moment we start being ourselves, confident of who we are, and pleased with who we have grown to be, then our thoughts will reflect this. Since thoughts are electromagnetic fields, they will spread around. And that's how others receive the vibe we release about ourselves. When we feel good about ourselves, others start feeling good in the presence of our electromagnetic energy, when we feel confident, others start feeling the same about our ideas and care about our opinions.

When I realized this, I started to use the same strategy with my clients as a life coach. One of my recent clients, Joanna, is looking for a companion, but it seems to be hard for her to attract someone. When she first told me this, I almost burst laughing.

She is very sexy lady, why is she having a hard time with this? I thought. She was very well dressed, her makeup was perfect, she seemed very confident, and she has a perfect body shape and weight. What was she talking about?

Then I realized that when it comes to relationships, she had a fear that she was not good enough.

This fear has its roots in the past and it's the result of bad experiences. So I had to work with Joanne to start loving herself first. The first step was to accept herself as she is. She is who she is for a reason, so I helped her find her reasons. Our reasons are usually hidden in our true desires, which we almost always push away as unworthy. Then I helped her forgive herself for any past mistakes or failed relationships.

Now she is ready to date again. With some tips on how to rock the first date, Joanne is on the go. She feels confident about her sexuality and happy to be with people. She no longer harbors fears about being undesirable.

The three stages that I used with Joanne were "Love yourself, Accept yourself, and Forgive yourself" I explain these in my book, Secret Beyond the Secret.

Sexy is a State of Mind
By Elle Sompres

Sexy was one of those words I didn't feel I could relate to growing up. Pretty? Perhaps Attractive? Sure. But sexy seemed like something else. Something exotic. Something I didn't quite feel or exude. Sexy was bold, alluring, powerful, seductive. Oh sure, I wanted to be those things-but I felt more restricted than that. More mediocre. No one was ever going to refer to me as "Sexy"-that's just not the right descriptor for this girl.

In high school, I even recall my best friend's mom describing our group of girlfriends as a few of us sat around the dining room table. One was pretty, the other was sexy, one cute, another beautiful...and her word for me? Plain. Hmmmm. Not so flattering. I just remember staring at her in disbelief. Not that I didn't believe she was possibly right in her assessment, I just couldn't believe she actually said that to an impressionable teenager. Even at a young age, I knew that didn't seem very nice. Hadn't she ever watched Bambi? "If you can't say somethin' nice, don't say nothin' at all." Thanks, Thumper. I agree. But there it was. And the thing is, I loved this woman and she was wonderful to me in many ways...but that comment stuck to me like glue.

It's strange how we carry things like that with us. Then they become our "story"...often times turning into our own personal truth. From a teen's point of view, if a woman who adores me sees me that way; the rest of the world must, as well. Right? So that must be the truth. Sexy? Nope-that definitely wasn't me.

I began looking for what I DID believe was sexy. The girl she had described in our group was definitely exotic-dark, ethnic, boys always paid attention to her. Shoot, even girls paid attention to her. She was that "girls want to be her & guys want to be with her" type of female. I still didn't feel like that was me.

I even went through a phase a bit later in life where I tried to show off my "assets" more in order to be seen as sexy. To be wanted…coveted… desired. But it wasn't the kind of attention I wanted. I wanted someone to see me as beautiful-but, most importantly, I wanted them to see my beautiful spirit and my beautiful heart.

And that's when it clicked. I began to see that sex appeal is not strictly based on appearance. I'm an attractive woman but there are always those who are prettier. But sexy isn't always the most physically appealing woman (or man) in the room anyway! It's more than that. Being sexy is a state of mind…a demeanor. A belief we hold about ourselves that we radiate outward. In a nutshell, I came to recognize that self love was the real door to sexy.

As I learned how to let go of the judgements I held over myself (and the assessments I felt others had made about me, as well), I have gotten more in touch with my real essence. And THAT is sexy! I had to release the feeling of not being good enough. Isn't that a big one for many of us? As a life coach I've come to learn that it most definitely is! But good enough for what? Or for whom? The ONLY person I need to be good enough for…is me. And when I believe in myself, show compassion to myself, behave lovingly towards myself, offer myself kindness & treat myself respectfully—well, that is what is truly sexy. That breeds confidence & the ability to live life with an open heart. I'm not sure I can think of anything sexier than that.

Olympic Triathlon at Pacific Grove
By Nobuko Sezaki

Why did I compete for the Olympic Triathlon?

Fostering self-confidence, the can-do spirit and eagerness to do one's best is what set Triathlons apart from other sports where winning seems to be what matters most.

Competing in a triathlon for me had nothing to do with being competitive. It was a competition within me to achieve my personal goals. Being unemployed I needed discipline and structure. Being overweight I needed to become fit and healthy. More importantly I missed a good challenge and building confidence. "Pure sexiness" comes from happiness that you build through overcoming challenges, and appreciating and respecting yourself.

The intense training put me in zones of discomfort and introduced me to a journey of unknown. September 12 marked my first day to complete an Olympic distance triathlon. The race was successful and took place surrounding Lovers Point in Pacific Grove just North of Carmel.

If one asks me what it was like to cross the finish line, the moment was the intense, exhilarating joy of feeling accomplished and confident. It was evidence of my achievement. That is pure sexiness. Here is how my story goes.

Training
Training began in February when my good friend, Diana, started inviting me for short runs. Having not lost much pregnancy weight after my delivery last September, I felt totally exhausted running one or two miles. Approaching the end of June, I was able to run five miles comfortably.

Swimming was my weakest area and it took a long time to improve. A few friends came out to help me improve my swim time. Jeremy swam with me at the Foster City lagoon. Gladys and I swam once a week in Redwood shores. Win, despite her demanding medical career, made a point to swim with me in San Mateo. Diana, Jeff, Ashley and I swam at Cowells Beach in Santa Cruz. By the end of July, I was comfortably able to swim for a mile and half.

The Race Day

At 7am Pacific Grove was drizzling wet and cold as expected. At 7:43am I set up my bike, affixed my bib numbers to my bike/helmet and got body marked. I saw large patches of dense kelp covering the majority of the route from the lookout area and became skeptical and concerned about the swim.

Fifteen minutes before my wave began I slowly stepped into the cold water for a warm-up swim. The water temperature was warmer than expected and that gave me some encouragement.

At 9:15am the MC counted down from ten and the blue caps rushed into the ocean. Swimming through kelp was annoying and difficult. A large number of athletes passed me within 200 yards of the start. I stopped a few times to get rid of the kelp tangling around my left leg. Drinking excessive amounts of ocean water and swimming against the current exerted my body.

Though feeling worn out by the end of the first loop I was lifted by a familiar face which popped before my eyes. Seeing Gladys waving both of her hands yelled my name repeatedly, I managed to finish the last swim portion.

Feeling beat, I slowly walked to the bike transition. Right when I put my bike shoes and helmet on, Jeff came to cheer me on. "Great job, I am proud of you!" Although my stomach was bloated due to excess amounts of water that I drank during the swim, breathtaking views of the wave splashing against cliffs took my mind off of the discomfort for a while.

By the time when I finished the second loop, I vomited most of the salt water and felt much better. I saved my legs for a run and enjoyed the picturesque view of the ocean.

Right before starting third loop I heard someone calling my name. Seeing Gerard pointing his i-phone at me brightened up my spirit.

Back to the transition, I changed to running shoes and put my cap on, I ran to the run out area. My mom, Gladys and Gerard yelled my name and saw me off to the first run loop. Running was much more comfortable than expected. I started counting numbers from 1 to 100 at every two steps to keep my mind occupied.

At the count 48, I stopped at the first aid station and asked for a big shower. Three cups of water were poured onto my cap. The historical yellow mansion surrounded by countless numbers of windows kept my attention.

At the count 97 passing by my mom vigorously waving her hands I took off for a second loop. Continuing to feel comfortable and strong, I finished the second loop. "This is it, I am almost done!" The guys at the same aids station ran at my pace and splashed a few cups of water over my head without being requested. "Great job 1045, almost there!"

As I approached the immense blue banners marking the finish, I wanted to cry. I wanted the moment to last forever since it took me a very long time to reach this point. As I crossed the finish line, a medal was immediately put over my neck.

Jeff immediately came to congratulate my achievement. I slapped high fives to Gladys and Gerard and then approached my mom. "Honey, we must change Jayden's diaper" was her first statement. "How about congratulations, Mom?" said I. Laughing hard, she told me how proud she felt to see me complete the race.

Beside the swim portion I felt strong throughout the race. My supportive team, the weather and scenic view made the event successful and memorable.

Special Thanks:
In looking back at the large wheels slowly rolling down, I am humbled and fortunate to have such awesome friends who made this experience successful and rewarding. I take my hat off to Gladys and Diana for inviting me to step into a transformative path of determination, discipline and challenge.

Honestly I wouldn't have participated in many of the beginning workouts without their presence and encouragement. Julian provided me with a customized 12 week effective training schedule and that helped improve my swim time tremendously.

Thank you to Win, for joining a few open water swims at Redwood Shores despite her outrageously intense residency program. I appreciate Yoko, Richard, Gerard, and Gladys for getting up before dawn and supporting my event(s).Seeing and hearing their cheers at each time lifted my spirits and convinced me to complete each race. I thank Jeff for his full support throughout my training and races. Every night he listened to my training updates and gave me tips and encouragement. I had nothing to prove by finishing the race.

Achieving "pure sexiness" comes from the experience of overcoming my physical and personal barriers, testing my limits and growing from the inner strengths. As a result, I've learned to respect and appreciate my healthy body and mind feeling completely sexy inside.

I would have never reached this goal without my friends' and family's tremendous support and encouragement. I've lost twenty three pounds since February. Someday I would like to share these amazing experiences with Jayden hoping that he and I could complete a race together.

Sexy Secret? Simple…Sacredness!
By Regiane Gorski

What makes me feel sexy?…First I thought: "men make me feel sexy"; but immediately I realized, that is not always true! Some, men, not all men, can be so insecure, that if they find a woman who is so beautiful, so sexy and so powerful, they will try bringing her down. When this is the case, men can have the opposite effect; if a woman is feeling down, she is not feeling sexy. The ways in which this can happen are individualized according to what each woman needs and what makes her happy or sad.

For me, if a man is unfaithful, deceitful, dishonest, and just to mention a few things; this turns me off completely. That man for a moment may succeed in having me doubt my self-worth and my "sexiness". So, depending on a man to make me feel sexy is putting too much power in a man's hands to determine how I feel…so, no!!! It would take a truly powerful man to be able to honor and cherish all that is in a woman. If I were to wait for such a man in order to feel sexy, that could take forever!!!

It is much better to find a way to feel sexy no matter what. If this man appears, great! That's a bonus…What makes me feel sexy is entirely up to me. I can feel and see myself as sexy without any outside affirmation from a man or from the media. Simple things, such as doing yoga, or taking walks put me in touch with my physical body. I feel sexy when I exercise, when I get in touch with my life force, when I am in nature, when I eat healthy and respect my body, these are things which make me feel alive and full of energy. It is when I have extra energy to spare and enjoy the beauty of life, that I feel sexy. So no junk food! No drugs! No booze.

Just as important as what I allow in my body, is what I say into the Universe. If I get into relationships and situations that stress me, I may be tempted to speak in anger. However, words can come back to bite me and create ugly scenarios as the backdrop of my life. I need harmony and peace to feel sexy. That doesn't mean that I won't say what needs to be said, but how and when I say it can make a big difference. Waiting to say something when I feel calm will allow me to express myself with grace, instead of anger, and will have a more powerful result-one that I won't regret....

Another very important factor in feeling sexy for me is my connection with the "Universe". Call it what you will, the Divine, God, Love, etc… Anyone and anything who stresses me is not helping me to stay in touch with that greater Life Source and is not contributing with my sexiness. Consequently, I walk away from people and situations that have too much drama, or that I am not in alignment with, such as people who are drunk, drugged or extremely self-centered. I do not let these people be a part of my innermost life and heart. I give them little to no time. My connection with the Divine is first and foremost! No one comes in between that! That connection is really the most powerful one and keeps me radiating some incredible magic from within. No toxic people!

For me, feeling sexy has to do with how I am flowing with life. Choosing my thoughts and words and associations, even choosing to watch only uplifting movies and TV shows, helps to keep the flow positive. I stay away from the mundane. For me feeling sexy is knowing that I am a Goddess just because I am a woman. Feeling sexy is staying away from the profane and always knowing that being a woman and being a sexy woman is being sacred.

Chapter 2

Sexy is the Fugitive from the Red Carpet

"Man is like a hunter.
When a woman is
completely naked
she looks a prey
that has already been caught."
~ Anonymous

"What a man most enjoys
about a woman's clothes
are his fantasies of how
she would look without them."
~ Brendan Francis

"For lingerie-inspired looks,
what matters is that
you convey an idea
of the unseen
and allow the dream."
- Stefano Gabbana

"There's the theory
that nudity doesn't really
make something sexy;
the characters
and their relationship
make it sexy."
~ Tim Robbins

Once when my boy-friend came to picked me up, he stepped out of the car and realized that he had forgotten to bring his wallet. Instantly, he felt very uncomfortable. He said, "I feel naked without my wallet!" I was so carried away with his feeling! What is the thing you can't live without? Have you ever feel that way when something is missing and you feel "naked"? Some say, "Make-up!" I remember Lady Gaga said, "My high heel shoes!" *Feeling naked* is the feeling of shame, lack of power and embarrassment. How can we work on empowering ourselves so that we feel brilliant and confident even when we forget to bring our wallet?

Robin Sharma was interviewed by Darren Hardy, publisher of the Success Magazine, to share his insight about living a well-rounded life of excellence. I love his "Michelangelo's metaphor". When Michelangelo faced the huge block of marble, what he saw, was his sculpture of "David". He had a clear vision of how the perfect "David" would look when he chipped away any part that didn't belong as part of his masterpiece.

I like to apply the concept of "Michelangelo's metaphor" to ourselves. Next time when you stand in front of the mirror, you should have a clear vision that what you are seeing is a masterpiece of art! No one in this world has your features, your body, your mind or your soul. You are unique! You are one of a kind! You are the *LIMTED EDITION*! Chip away any misperception of yourself or any self-criticism. Never down-talk yourself that you are not pretty enough; you are not slim enough; you are not tall enough; you are not tanned enough; you are not young enough; you are not smart enough…get rid of all the excuses. Don't be another giraffe shopping for high heel shoes! Focus on what we have, instead of what we don't have. You are well equipped, with the right features, right height and right body. Recognize yourself as a perfect YOU, chip away all the negativities.

I went to a seminar a while ago. The room was filled with people. When the presenter brought something up, there was a middle aged woman who sat a few rows behind me, who suddenly burst out crying.

The speaker asked her why she was so emotional, what was the reason for her tears? She said that she was 50 years old and time was ticking. She didn't feel like she had achieved anything. My first instinct was, "50 are still very young!" Also, she didn't think that she was special. Well, I mentally told her that she is special, there is absolutely no other like her. She has her unique physical features with her unique personality, mind and soul. There is no one in this world has her DNA. In fact, the speaker said something very interesting. He gave the example of Ronald Regan becoming President of the United States of America when he was 70 years old and he is considered to be one of the most respected presidents. Why is she worried about being 50?

I am a mother of two awesome young gentlemen. I learned from my mother that I have to love my children unconditionally. Yes, I do! This is what nature intended, so it is not hard to do. But with my 24 years of experience working in the lingerie business; having the opportunity to work with nearly naked women day in and day out; helped me to realize that many women, although they love their children unconditionally, they are not able to do the same for themselves. On the contrary, they beat themselves up constantly.

I met a gorgeous woman at a seminar. She came to introduce herself to me. Soon, our conversation turned to "the lingerie", as you can imagine. She told me that she could not look at herself in the mirror. She described her body as "disgusting"! I was so shocked! She was not only a gorgeous woman with an hour glass body shape, but she was tastefully dressed too! I could not believe how she criticized herself! I started to tell her to stop demeaning herself. She was frozen for a while, and then she calmed down and started to listen to me. I looked through her sparkling eyes and said, "Think of the person who said the meanest thing to you-Do you have that person in mind yet?" I gave her a few seconds to picture that person in her mind. Then I said firmly, "You are way meaner than that person! You will not say that to anyone, right? So why do you say that to yourself? Stop putting yourself down! From now on, you have to program your head with positive thought of yourself. You need to look at the mirror and start convincing yourself that every single part of yourself is a master piece. Stop condemning yourself and start praising of what you already equipped.

You might say that it is easier said than done. Tell me about it, I have been there and done that. I was raised under the influence of the Chinese humble attitude; we were not to speak of our own accomplishments. My mother would never say anything positive about me in front of my aunts, uncles and friends, but she would easily praise my cousins' achievements. That was the way to show that we were humble and educated. I am not judging whether that way is right or wrong, I just want to draw attention to the fact that Eastern culture is very different from Western culture.

It used to be that if anyone gave me a compliment, I would feel so uncomfortable and so guilty that I wanted to hide. My normal reaction would be to say something bad about myself so as to deflect the compliment. For example, there was a young colleague of mine, who ran into me by the copying machine. She said to me, "I want to be you one day!" I felt so uncomfortable that I answered with self deprecation, "What? You want to be five feet tall?" I am short, so that was the way for me to escape the compliment.

I gradually adapted to the Western mentality while I was working in Toronto, Canada. I started to realize that there is no shame in acknowledging our own achievement; no shame in self-love; no shame in telling others how great your children are; no shame on praising how much your loved one pampers you…these are what we call *"share the joy"* in Western society. If someone gives a compliment to me, I just simply accept it by saying, "Thank you!" with a big smile.

In fact, it was quite an experience for me when I first visited a Soroptimist's meeting. When you donate some money, you can have one minute to brag about anything you want to share amongst the group. Some talked about how their business improved; another talked about her daughter's winning at the athletic competition…it was so new to me. We don't need to be ashamed of our achievements. We share the joy because others want to hear that you did well too. It is encouraging and up-lifting.

It seems so simple and not a big deal, but believe me, it took me a good while before I could put my up-bringing behind and adopt a completely different mentality. It is all about recognizing the worthiness within yourself and acknowledging it. Now that I am in Western society, I really think that it is important. It should be true across all cultures.

If you have a hard time recognizing your worthiness, I suggest you do it by starting from the deepest layer of yourself-your mind! It's worth trying the following method: Stand in front of the mirror and see beyond the surface. Remember *"Michelangelo's metaphor"*? Think of the Dream YOU and start to visualize all of the great qualities of your Dream YOU coming to the surface and manifesting themselves! Compliment yourself everyday by adding a new great quality that you have been longing for.

Chip away the insecurities, the pain and the shame. Christina Aguilera's song "Beautiful" says it best-*"I am beautiful no matter what they say. Words can't bring me down. I am beautiful in every single way."* Orchestrate the thought of being blessed, being talented, being valuable and being confident in your mind. Re-wire your negative thoughts. You don't need to make everyone like you. You don't need anyone's approval. If you can start to love yourself unconditionally, the beauty and sexiness in you will come through and transformation will take place.

Dress for no one but yourself
Whenever I meet someone new, I introduce myself as a lingerie designer. Most of the women will give me a sad face and say, "Too bad! I don't have a boy-friend!" Really, you only dress for your

boy-friend? You cannot dress up for yourself? I think you owe it to yourself. I always liked to role play in front of the mirror when I was a teenager. I dressed to please myself. I felt so good knowing I can turn heads when I walk down the street. It boosts my confidence and self esteem. I have no need to conform to social standards; I can be truly responsible for being ME!

Role playing makes me think of Halloween. The moment we dress as some characters, we turn into a different person. When we dress up like a pirate, we are suddenly strong and powerful. When we dress like Dorothy in the "Wiz of Ox", we turn into a sweet innocent girl. When we dress up like a sexy pin up doll, we feel sexy inside and out. Human thought is very powerful. It can break or build our personality.

Never change yourself for someone else. They might betray you; but you will never betray yourself. When you meet the one who is truly in love with you; he will love you as you are, not the modified you.

Law of Attraction

My friend, a Psychology professor, Ardiana Bani Cohn, once told a story about how human minds are attracted by the unseen, which can convey an idea, arouse the imagination and thus build their dreams. The story about how love first started goes like this:

"At the time when people all lived in big groups and walked around naked, one of the girls threw a sheep's skin over her shoulder, unintentionally, and continued on her way. Just because some part of her body was covered, it made her seem more mysterious and more desirable to the men, who started to fight for her attention."

Same as Christina Aguilera's belief, I guess there is a fine line between a natural sexiness which is the "real sexy"; and the "trying too hard to be sexy" which is not really sexy. All those tips about "sensually playing with the tips of your hair" or "throwing a sexy eye signal" are never really sexy because they are "intentional acts".

The real sexy is a combination of your external and internal beauty. The external beauty is your attire-that means the whole package from head to toe. When one knows how to dress herself to emphasize the very best of her body, complementing her skin color and her personality, she is a Fashion Victor. But focusing just on the outer package will not hold the attention for a long period of time. Revealing too much is never sexy! Also, trying too hard to get noticed is a big mistake.

As Ardiana said, "Being yourself and happy in your own skin makes men go crazy about you." The ultimate sexiness should come naturally from your inner self. If you are able to present yourself with confidence, it will speak volumes about who you are.

In my blog "Lingerissimi.com–An intellectual dimension within the world of lingerie", I had over a hundred of articles about lingerie, fashion and art. One of the top five articles is "The Law of Attraction". Throughout the different eras and geographic locations, scientists have proven that the mystery surrounding the "seen" and "unseen" draws in the intense curiosity of the human mind. The partially covered body piques the curiosity. What can be seen is already out there, so our mind is triggered by the part that is covered.

When people think of what I do as a lingerie designer, they immediately think of sexy lingerie, sexy body, nudity...well, that's obvious. I deal with many real women every day, different sizes, different shapes, different colors, different ages...but the most interesting thing is their minds-how they view themselves inspires me to explore the human mind.

People don't always understand why I choose to be a lingerie designer. They think that lingerie is something that no one sees, so who cares? The fact is, everyone sees it. The one wearing it knows it and that's effects how she feels about herself and relates to others. The unseen is so arousing, so mysterious.

Take control of your destiny

Your purpose in life is not to live up to someone else's dream. You don't need to be the conformer on the Red carpet, be a fugitive if you have to. I remember a colleague of mine told me a story about her little sister. As a child, her mother always wanted to play piano, but never had the chance. So she wanted her sister to learn piano. Her little sister did not like it but she could not refuse. Eighteen summers passed by and she finally got to the highest level in piano. The day she received her certificate, she told her mother, "Now that I've fulfilled your dream, from this moment on, I am not going to touch the piano anymore!" She hasn't played piano since! It is sad that we spent our lives only in living someone else's dream, meeting other's expectations.

No one should be responsible for our lives and we should not be responsible for other's lives either. Take control of your own destiny!

Fedora & Cane?
By Nicole

I loved to play dress up as a child. I remember bursting from my bedroom with a blanket over my head and dragging my mother's high heels on my feet-I was a beautiful bride waltzing down a grand aisle. Dream weddings like this are held in bedrooms and hallways all over the world.

Years passed and I still love to dress up. Just as my feet grew bigger than my mother's, dress up evolved beyond the boundaries of child's play.

When I feel down, I say to myself, "Enough! You are better than this, don't be a shit. Don't be sad, don't be jealous…it's time to be awesome!" I search for the inspiration of the day. Who do I want to be? Lately, I love the strong image of Janet Jackson dancing in a black and white suit with a fedora. Some days, I want to become a sweet Disney princess with rosy cheeks and a pretty dress; or that beautiful woman who does housework in a headscarf, earrings, and espadrilles…so real, so down-to-earth, and so fabulous! This can change from day to day, and inspiration can come from anywhere. Play a bit of dress up and become this image that I am admiring. Fantasy is an easy escape from dull moments. Dress up transforms the way I look and the way I feel.

Maybe this is silly but sometimes I would do this even if I have nowhere to go. Just dig around in my closet, and play with the makeup that I don't regularly use. The best part is, I can be as outrageous and experimental as I want! I can try bold colorful make-up looks like I'm part of carnival in Brazil, why not? Nobody's around to judge. If I fail and find a ridiculous clown in the mirror, I have all the time in the world to refine the look, or simply laugh it off and wind down with a refreshing shower. But every now and then, I discover a GREAT look.

There is no storybook ball gown or Cat Woman's leather hooded bodysuit; or bold hair and makeup from a futuristic blockbuster movie buried in my closet. The treasures I find are these fantastic personality-inspired looks that use unexpected combinations of pieces I already own.

Then, I find the perfect occasion to go all out! Birthdays, New Year parties, girls' night outs are all opportunities to OVERDRESS! It's ok to be playful and dramatic. And on lucky days, I manage to convince my friends to dress up in the same theme. The theme is sometime hotly debated, but whatever we agree on, we always have a fun, memorable time.

What's in it with those sexy women?
By Anonymous

My first thoughts about the subject of being sexy is that some of the sexiest women I have known were not the most beautiful I have known. Therefore, being sexy does not require you to be beautiful. Grooming, dress, makeup and personality can be the most important things.

Ah, yes, and then there's the subject of lovemaking. A great lover is always sexy and it is rather difficult to explain but the way a woman touches me and flirts with me and acts like it's going to be so much fun to be with me all play a part. And it always helps if she laughs at my jokes!

A few examples are in order. One of the sexiest women I have known was one I dated in my 20's when I had a lot of access to a lot of women. Let's call her Karen for the sake of this chapter. Karen was NOT beautiful and quite frankly wore too much makeup. But she was well groomed, dressed in some very sexy outfits and gave me a lot of attention. She was also very feminine. I think most men look for femininity in a woman and that's where opposites (masculinity and femininity) attract each other.

Karen would also do some special things. When she knew I would be spending the night she would get out her best satin sheets for the bed. She would touch me often during our time together and sometimes it was so soft and gentle that I would barely notice it. Sometimes she would whisper into my ear with her lips gently touching my ear. NOW THAT'S SEXY!

Another woman I knew, Geri, was not that good looking and somewhat overweight but she was a wonderful lover who was willing to explore many different ways of lovemaking. And I could tell she really enjoyed it, she wasn't faking it (or if she was she was really super at faking it). But whenever I left her I felt so fulfilled from our lovemaking that I was floating on air for the rest of the day or night.

It can be the little things that are so important when becoming sexy. One woman I dated always kept her nails in great condition and her lovely red nail polish looked great. And she had beautiful blonde hair running down past her shoulders. However, once we started "going together" she used nail polish less often and cut her hair quite short, and frankly, I then didn't see her as that sexy anymore. But a lot of it had to do with her attitude, not just her grooming—you see, I didn't feel as important to her when she didn't continue with the nail polish and longer hair thing—she was really much more into her career than me (More so than the average woman).

I suppose that most of us men just want to feel needed and important to a woman. When I say needed, I mean mostly on a psychological level. And we need the woman too, to be happier and feel like love is shared between us.

I am thinking of another woman I used to work with. She was average looking and slightly overweight BUT SHE WAS SUPERB WHEN IT CAME TO APPLYING MAKEUP AND SHE REALLY LOOKED APPEALING. She also dressed very well. We never dated but she did end up marrying a very successful man. So, applying makeup correctly can go a long way in how appealing a woman is.

A terrific personality can also play a big role in how a woman is perceived. A woman who is personable (not overly aggressive though) can attract men who find her sexy because she always seems to say the right thing at the right time, has a sense of humor and does not embarrass the man when out in public. One time when I was on a date the woman said in a loud voice in a crowded restaurant, "Let's go home and get naked!" I was all for the idea but did not appreciate her announcing this to everyone else in the restaurant. That relationship was short-lived.

Well, I know I could wax on about all the other things men find sexy about women but all this writing about the subject has me rather stirred up so I need to go home and take a cold shower.

Sexy From the Inside Out
By Sheryl Robinson

My first attraction to "sexy" was the cover of an Herb Alpert and the Tijuana Brass album called "Whipped Cream." It showed a woman covered with just that, barely covering her breasts and the rest of her body. I was too young to know anything about sex, but I was drawn to that cover…I wanted to be that girl!

I grew up when Christie Brinkley and Cindy Crawford were the epitome of beautiful, and "sexy" was narrowly defined…not much room for the rest of us who didn't fit that mold.

I had long legs but a short torso, a slightly crooked nose, nice hair, pretty eyes, flat butt, belly too loose even as a teenager when most teenagers have a nice flat one. My older sisters didn't wear make-up or pay attention to their clothes and I felt self-conscious trying to figure those things out myself.

I had thoughts and desires about sex and wanted a boyfriend, but was a bit overweight and other than dating occasionally, I didn't have a full-fledged relationship until I met my ex-husband when I was 21.

I had been so awkward before I met him, but I fell in love and thought we would live happily ever after. We had a long distance relationship for two years before we got married, so we only had sex every few weeks because that's how often we saw each other. I was thrilled to get married because in addition to building a life with the man I loved, I thought I'd finally have a normal sex life!

I was surprised to find my 28 year old husband wasn't very interested in sex and we still only had a physical relationship every few weeks even though we slept in the same bed every night. My sexual curiosity was running rampant, but my confidence wasn't very high. I wasn't very experienced, but I wanted to explore and I thought every man wanted to have sex all the time, so I thought the lack of activity meant the problem must be with me. I wasn't perfect. I didn't have a perfect body or a perfect face, so I read books to find out what to do and how to do it, and I asked him to share what his fantasies were so I could entice him, and yet, I still found myself left alone almost every night-longing for my husband to touch me and make love with me.

Fast forward 20 years and two children later-I had gained and then lost a lot of weight, and now men came onto me over and over again, telling me they wished their wives were like me and how awesome I was and how sexy-and I started feeling like an attractive and desired woman…but I needed more, I needed to feel sexy through my own eyes, not through the eyes of a man.

I needed to feel beautiful from the inside out, so I made an appointment to have some photographs taken just for me, and I started working out and eating better and more weight dropped off and I felt muscles in places I didn't remember having them before!

I went to a lingerie shop and for the first time in my life, spent two hours trying on one outfit after another, pretty panties and bras and robes and bustiers, silky, soft lingerie in black lace and turquoise blue satin and white and green and hot pink! I felt like I was in a movie–and those pretty pieces of fabric made me feel sexy and beautiful even when I was all by myself. I vowed I would never wear ugly underthings again…I wanted to feel this beautiful and sexy, even if no one but me knew I had them on. I loved wearing thigh hi's and showing off my long legs-one of my best features, and I felt a surging confidence I never had before.

Shortly before my photo shoot, I separated from my husband after too many unhappy years, and almost a year later, met an incredibly sexy man a couple of years older than me who can't keep his hands off me. He loves how much I love sex, how feminine, yet strong, I am, how I always wear pretty things, and he's always looking at me as though he's taking my clothes off. At 48 my life feels like it's just beginning, and my hot boyfriend makes me feel like I'm the sexiest woman alive.

Time To Turn The Lights On
By Adryenn Ashley

Who can forget Teri Hatcher doing those impossible splits right on the studio floor on Oprah? Or Carmen Electra positively gushing about what exotic dance has done for her body and bedroom tactics? A large number of celebrities have recently taken to a sexy alternative to working out, from pole vaulting they have leapt straight to pole dancing. And they aren't stopping at pole-dancing! Our celebrity pin-up girls have been everywhere and done everything, from Strip-Aerobics to Exotic Dance Work Outs, the motto seems to be 'Everything sexy goes'!

If this entire gush for sex is making you blush, you go ahead and click your tongue and hang your head in shame, and no one will begrudge you. "SEX SELLS" and we are being sold it morning, noon and night through every possible channel. It screams at you from gigantic billboards featuring gorgeous demi-love-gods. It pierces into your fantasy's through the television and fondles your imagination with semi-naked bodies scattered all over the net. Living in the USA is, in itself, like one giant, prolonged orgasm…and as a woman, the marketing message you hear every day is that you are expected to idolize those models and endeavor to look like one.

Sure you wanna be Carrie from "Sex and the City" and moan and groan and roll around on your bed with a different guy every night, seven nights a week turning your life into a series of fantastic sexual escapades…but you'll snap out of it, after all life is not a TV show, and learning how to embrace your sexuality takes time and effort.

In America amidst the glamour of the TV shows and the supposed sexual abandonment, the skin and the G-Strings (even on Bratz dolls), we women have to deal with mixed messages, guilt trips, religious dogma, body image, and misinformation. Sure getting your hymen snapped by

16 is a must(???), but so is regretting doing it by 25. Beneath all of our external frills, getting laid is an issue we women deal with badly.

The concept of 'Positive Sex' is an idea not many of us have managed to fathom yet. Fornication is still, essentially a male domain, where we women participate like whimpering goats, hesitating and interestingly enough feeling insecure about our role in it all.

A majority of women I know swear by making love in the dark. 'It's romantic' they coo when I ask them the point of that. Here's what I KNOW, most of us are ashamed of our body. Nudity is a concept we haven't been taught to handle well. Seeing ourselves naked freaks us out, and knowing that someone else is watching us naked, desiring our body for itself, brings to life our worst fears. This is the gaze our parents warned us against, this is what Church lessons have told us to avoid. So off goes the light, plunging everything, from ourselves, to that desirous gaze, to our insecurities, into comforting darkness.

The truth is that the darkness serves as a warm invitation to what Susan Bremer calls our 'Shadow" side. 'Every woman wants to take a trip to their wild side" she explains, 'We all yearn to seduce. But we've been told over and over again that to rejoice in our body is immoral, yet the wish to feel powerful in our sensuality, to express our sexuality remains." Susan, a proud 'Gentleman club' dancer considers her sexual prowess to be her way of establishing her role in a world hounded by men. "When I'm at work," she says "I'm surrounded by men in coats and ties—bosses and underlings, jocks and nerds. All of them are the kinds of men who made me feel small. But now I can reduce the top dog to a lapdog by staring at him, opening my top, and smiling".

This incredible sense of power needs some delving into. I'm not advocating that you go get a second job as a stripper, but understanding what you need to feel powerful and secure is a worthy pursuit. As women, all of us suffer from our own insecurities. It's a cliché by now but they all say that the world belongs to the testosterone thugs. They keep us down everywhere, be it in our boardroom or our bedroom. And slowly we grow used to being kept down, such that we soon we are conditioned to not reversing the situation at all. But the truth is, we hold the power. All of it. The story that we are helpless is a lie. And realizing and basking in your power, all of it, all of you, will set you free!

A positive sex-image, whether you use it or not, can and will alter the way you see the world most miraculously. Your sexual achievements in the bedroom can give you the kind of omnipotent confidence which oozes out from your personal to public sphere. For any woman with low self-esteem, the act of embracing your sexuality serves as a miracle tool for believing that she can have that effect on other people, in a non-sexual environment too. For me, wearing a sexy set of underwear that nobody can see was the gateway to transferring the power I felt in the bedroom to the rest of my life.

The thing is, much as we try to shake it off, we are all sexual beings, sex is important to us and it has the power to make us feel good, very good. The sad fact is that 65% of women in the US do not, at their heart of hearts, take this idea seriously. Good sex and an attempt to have good sex for them is still a nudge-nudge- whisper-whisper issue. This attitude gets transferred from them to their kids and grandkids and so on, such that each generation of these young women grow up with the idea that every time they are making love they ought to feel guilty about it. This mystifying of the subject is harmful for a lot of reasons. For starters it gives us a lifelong baggage of guilt, every time we think about sex, every time we fantasize or our hands itch to masturbate we feel like a criminal. The constant feeling that sex is wrong or dirty leads to a negative self-image as a person. That misinformation means that when we are in the act it can be hard to enjoy it, leading to severe sexual frustration, not a feeling you'd like to carry around with you.

This discussion might go on and on, because of our trouble to face the fact that we like getting laid. But let's just say, it all has a very easy solution. Get in to your sexiest lacy underwear, devote tonight to unleashing the temptress in you and for once really enjoy it without hang-ups. You will like the results tomorrow morning.

Chapter 3

Sexy is a Time Capsule

"It takes a long time to become young."
—**Pablo Picasso**

"Nobody grows old merely by living a number of years.
We grow old by deserting our ideals. Years may wrinkle
the skin, but to give up enthusiasm wrinkles the soul."
—**Samuel Ullman**

"Youth is the gift of nature, but age is the work of art."
—**Stanislaw Lec**

"There is a fountain of youth: it is your mind, your talents, the
creativity you bring to your life and the lives of people you love.
When you learn to tap this source, you will truly have defeated age."
—**Sophia Loren**

"Wrinkles should merely indicate where smiles have been."
—**Mark Twain**

49

When Helen Woo interviewed me during her internet radio show "Self-Aid Success Stories" earlier this year. We talked about "What is Sexy?" We received a phone call from a listener. She told me that she had just turned 40. She is a stay home mom and she also does "match-making" as her side thing. She told me that she has many clients that are over 40, over 50, and all feel that it's hard to find a soul-mate because they feel that they cannot compete with the young 20 year old girls. She asked me to give advice on how to gain confidence and win the men over.

Oh my! I have heard that before. In fact, I do know some single women who are looking for their life-time partners, but in vain! And they had the same concern!

I agree with Sophia Loren. Your mind, your talent and your creativity bring out the youth in you. The secret to winning men over is to truly understand the major qualities that men seek when they are looking for a soul-mate. Intelligent and confident individuals always attract people, no matter what is their age.

I think the root of this issue is the level of self-esteem. Low confidence brings low self-esteem. When you compare yourself unfavorably to others, it will cause you to withdraw, become shy and have difficulty in communicating with others, especially in large groups.

Obviously, personal development is a very important part of the solution. Read self-help books, attend seminars, learn from the greatest, listen to self-help CDs or programs, meditate, practice positive self-talk. Henry Ford once said, "Anyone who stops learning is old, whether at twenty or eighty. Anyone who keeps learning stays young. The greatest thing in life is to keep your mind young." One will have wrinkles while aging, but it doesn't define your inner quality. When you can see beyond your physical appearance, you will appreciate your true value.

Have you ever had someone gave you a compliment on your good looks and it instantly changed the way you saw yourself? You immediately lift up your chest, hold your head up high…if you understand the importance of self talk, it's time to plant that seed in your mind. Tell yourself that you are beautiful and sexy, from the inside and out. Nobody can take away from you.

Even the sexy Victoria Beckham was once quoted in Harper's Bazaar magazine, "The older you get, the more comfortable you become with yourself, and you accept what you have physically." So again, confidence is a major ingredient in being sexy. That is something more easily acquired through life experience.

Put your focus on what you have, not what you don't have. When you are able to infuse your attitude and your mind set with confidence, you will be able to attract anyone in your life.

Of course, a 40 or 50 year old woman cannot physically compete with a 20 year old girl. If you have to compete with them, the pressure will just wear you down. Instead of trying to measure up to them, why not think of the ways in which they cannot measure up to you? That is the deep intellectual level that can only be achieved with life experience.

I know that men, especially in their 40's, 50's, or even 60's, if they are looking for the life-time partner, they will appreciate a woman who has life experience too! They will appreciate someone who has a career, is driven, motivated, and has a sense of humor, confidence, is fun, patient and considerate. Now, a lot of these qualities come naturally through life experience.

Remember, men who look for these qualities in a woman are probably those who want to establish a long term relationship. They are most likely attracted by inner qualities than a pretty, naïve face, provocative outfit or make up. Men who are initially attracted by the outer package will eventually desire communication and supportiveness from their woman. If they cannot find those qualities in her, they might move on to someone else.

Also, I truly believe if you are desperately looking for a soul-mate, the pressure will make you look too needy! You may be too nervous, too demanding or even too fake! My advice is to relax, focus on friendship, enjoy the company, share some laughs. Having a positive attitude is the best! Let your vibe shine and win him over with your great personality! Develop a support system, be each other's cheer leader, be genuinely interested and be sympathetic! Don't always complain and whine about how hard life is. Don't talk about your past relationships. Men do not like to listen to those stories, especially in the beginning of a friendship or relationship.

Women today are very fortunate. Our status in society is much higher than before. We have careers, we are financially independent, we are educated, and we travel–leading to greater wisdom and increased communication skills. We have become more adept at expressing ourselves. As long as we have the attitude of being self-sufficient, having a partner is not what determines our happiness. If we happen to find them, they are there to enhance our happiness; without them, we are still happy. This kind of attitude will most likely lead us not only to find a man, but a GOOD MAN!

I remember when I had my last book signing event at the Luxe Lingerie at Beverly Hills. I met a very interesting woman. She was petite like me, about 60 years old and a kindergarten teacher. She was a big fan of lingerie and that is why she came to my book signing. She bought my book "Almost Naked"–Lingerie, Secret of the Guilty Pleasure. She told me how much she enjoys lingerie. She doesn't need a man, she is single and she enjoys pleasing herself. She put on her sexy lingerie and steps into her world of fantasy. She washes her dishes and vacuums her floor in her sexy lingerie and stiletto. She has a very pleasant personality and positive attitude. She is adorable and absolutely a lovely lady to chat with. She does not allow her age to hold her back from doing anything that she likes to do. She develops a good relationship with herself-and this is the very first step to inviting the right man into her life because she knows how to embrace the place where she is.

So be thankful for your age, not everyone can live up to your age. Aging gracefully as a woman is beautiful and very sexy. As we go through different stages in life, from childhood, to adult to becoming a strong individual to stepping into our golden age, enjoy different stages of life. Be grateful each day!

Transforming the Goddess…Unleashing Potential
By Rhonda Clure

When I was introduced to pole fitness…pole dancing, I thought it sounded like a lot of fun and why not give it a try right? Little did I know at the time, this experience would transform my life in so many profound and amazing ways, I could have never have imagined. Many of the amazing women in my life have been asking…"what exactly is this Inner Bombshell thing you're doing?" I thought I would tell you a little bit about this journey I've been on and how teaching pole and chair dance came into my life.

Almost three years ago I decided to finally take my dear friend Miyoko up on her offer to take a sexy fitness pole class. I knew about her classes and had wanted to check it out because it sounded like fun! We did a fun warm up and the girls took to the poles. Holy cow! I was blown away by the athleticism and strength these women had all while looking sexy and graceful, terms I would certainly not have use to describe myself. I was hooked after the first class and decided to jump in. I figured one class a week would be all I could do. I was never a girl who liked to go to the gym or be on a treadmill…dancing, no matter how awkward I felt, and was a lot more fun.

I was blown away by the spins and tricks these "youngsters" were able to do!! Being 47 years of age at the time…(not old) I can pretty much say I am the most "mature" student regularly attending class at the studio. Once a week turned into twice…up to four times a week! I just couldn't get enough of it. What I would discover is that my life was about to be transformed in the most amazing way I could have never expected.

Trying to embrace my now later 40's was a barrel of fun. Needless to say, I had gained a few pounds, and just felt run down and not particularly comfortable in my own skin. I know as women we ALL experience this!

It has nothing to do with age, size, etc., it's just something we, as women, deal with. The thing is we all think the women around us look like they have it all together and it's just "me" that experiences this sort of thing.

I began spending more and more time at the studio because I felt so comfortable and the other women accepted me for who I was…late 40s and about 20 pounds overweight and a little grumpy on occasion. It's easy to get stuck in our "stuff", the day to day junk that can wear you down. Every time I was in the studio I was encouraged and loved by my new "sisters".

In the beginning I watched these goddesses do all of these amazing things and although I was having fun I had convinced myself that I would never be able to do most of what I had seen these girls do, because I wasn't fit enough or young enough and whatever other excuses I made up in my head. Over time, I started getting stronger, doing some of those tricks and truly surprised myself! Of course, the girls had been encouraging me all along because they knew something I hadn't figured out yet, that the only limitations I had were those I created in my mind.

About a year into my new found addiction, Miyoko shared with us information about a competition in the Los Angeles area. I never would have considered it except that she said to me…"you should do this!" The beauty of being late 40's is that sometimes you just say to yourself, what the hell, I'll try it, what do I have to lose?…so I jumped in and faced my fears.

We also put together a team to perform a pole routine at the International Pole Convention! Never in a million years would I have ever…EVER…thought I would be doing anything like this! At the competition, I had the opportunity to watch and meet others from the pole fitness world and I was blown away by what they could do and how absolutely loving and supportive they all were. "Competitor's" were cheering each other on…truly amazing! Then I had a chance to watch the top people in the country perform…unbelievable! I had the privilege of watching one artist in particular, Greta. Everyone in the pole community knows who I am talking about. Greta did an amazing performance with some of the most bad ass moves I have ever seen. Guess what? She was 61 at the time. WOW! At that moment, I realized I had had all of these notions about what I could do, couldn't do and that she just blew all of my excuses out the window.

What had I been saying no to? There were moves I never even attempted because I just "knew" I could never do them. So I walk into the studio the Monday after this great experience and one the girls, who lovingly challenged me, turned and said…"you can do this"!!! So I tried this new thing, and I did it!! Well…shut the front door!! I realized, I had been saying no to try things in the studio and also in my life. What other ways had I been holding myself back from my greatest potential?

So here is where I take a huge breath and share something that only my closest friends know. I have been married for almost 28 years. I felt this relationship had stopped working more than 10 years ago. Every aspect of my life was perfect, except for this. I grew up in the Midwest, where the culture was to NOT discuss marital issues, and you count your blessings. Who am I to complain? I'm not going to start the blame game, really my spouse hasn't changed much at all, it was me that had changed and started to find my voice. I am not a victim; I was a participant in how things were and are between us. We grew to see things in very different ways, and I found myself living in this space where I felt like I wasn't honoring myself, and that that it was selfish of me to think I deserved something different. I lived in this space for so long. I lived in fear of jeopardizing the life we built for ourselves and our daughter. Every day I got up, went to work and for the most part I was very happy, but this discomfort started to become debilitating. I didn't want to put on a happy face when I wasn't feeling, well, happy. I was always the person other people lean on when they need help or comfort. It was harder to help others when I needed help too.

So what on earth does this have to do with pole dancing? Every morning in our women's only class, I would hear the other women's stories, some fun and joyful, others where they were struggling too. For a few months I listened to these women, a sort of validation that I wasn't crazy and that I certainly was not alone. And then it happened. I happened to stay a little longer after class with a couple of my closest friends from the studio and I shared what my life had been like the past 10 years. They embraced me, held and comforted me. I had such a huge burden lifted off of my shoulders simply by just sharing this for the first time. Over the past 3 years I have literally been transformed, my body, my mind and my spirit. This amazing community of women, true goddesses in every sense of the word, lifted me up, accepted and embraced me, so that I could start moving myself forward. I've moved past fears and I am surrounded by people who love and support me.

Anyone who knows me knows I am passionate about helping others, especially women. We have the power to make a huge positive impact on those around us and our world when we are sharing our talents and gifts with the world. I decided I needed to teach what I have learned to other women. Not that I am the best dancer…certainly not! What I see all the time is women, who are overwhelmed, run down, lack confidence and are not comfortable in their own skin. I've been there so I know exactly what that's like. I can see a woman from across the room that I know can benefit from what I have experienced. I want to help other women by sharing this experience with them and help them find the confidence to share their gifts and come into their power. I not only wanted but needed to help other women connect with that inner diva. I became a teacher so I could help other women discover what I have discovered. No matter what age, height or size, we are all beautiful women and can help each other discover and empower the goddess within us.

My Evolution as a Woman of Substance
By Nancy Ferrari

As I reflect on the chapters of my life, the word "sexy" had an entirely different meaning during my teen years, as being sexy was based on the illusion and observation of actresses and models displayed in magazines or in movies. As I evolved through my teen years, a challenging time of discovering our identity, I found myself being defined by someone else's opinions, saying "yes" when I wanted to say "no", and striving to meet other's expectations of perfection, all of which ultimately labeled me as being "sexy".

I realized quickly that it was all about my physical appearance that was created for me by a modeling agency. I recall the director of the agency telling me what to wear, how to walk, what to say, when to say it, and altered my appearance with a more mature appearance, creating the illusion of looking as if I was 21 years old when I was only 16. I felt that with each change, I was giving away my personal power as I was being groomed for success in the modeling, beauty pageant and entertainment industry.

I was crowned Miss North Hollywood, which shifted my focus as a high school student into an adult world which further challenged my identity. Although it was a great experience, I observed that much of the glitz and glamour was an illusion, and it was time to discover my true and authentic self.

What I discovered was a new definition of my identity and learned that being a sexy and sensual woman was all about innate charisma, magnetism and the gifts of a natural beauty. I separated myself from the stigma of others' definition of sexy and stepped into my personal empowerment and honored my natural gifts as a young woman.

A role model for me was Sophia Loren, as she naturally exuded the qualities as a woman of substance, always exquisite in every way.

Through these observations and reflections, I realized that I didn't have to <u>try</u> to be sexy anymore. It was always within me and I still exude the same natural characteristics as I grow older and embrace my sensuality more than ever.

With age comes wisdom and my husband of 34 years reminds me that I will always be a woman of substance as my inner and outer beauty continues to radiate outward. The shift of honoring the essence of me, focusing on being healthy and fit, and sharing my life experiences is far more rewarding as I am in alignment with my values within my body, mind and spirit.

In summary, the word sexy is all about how we feel inside and out and when a woman is connected with her true and authentic self, confidence is what is seen and felt by others. I no longer measure myself by anyone else's standards as I am a confident and sexy woman of substance!

Sizzzlin' Sexy at Sixty
By Suzy Manning

As I engage with myself and life in my sixties, I feel empowered, wise, and sexy. At sixty, sexy is an inner knowing that I have intuitive wisdom to share with the world, a sense of self that sends vibrations of electricity into a room when I enter, and humor to laugh at myself when I take me or life too seriously. Sexy comes from within my core. It is a feeling of self-worth, self-confidence, and self-love. It is love of all of life knowing that we are all connected in this web that we weave.

Sexy at sixty says I choose to speak my truth. I stand up for what is not working in my life and in the world. I embrace what resonates in my heart, co-create with other wise women, and lead from a space of empowerment, collaboration, abundance, and inclusivity.

Sexy is a brilliant radiance that comes from within when I own my magnificence. Once I ignite this spark within, I can wear anything and I will attract others to me. Often, others think they are attracted to you because of your fashion statement, your career, or your social status, but it is the inner energy that draws others to you like a magnet. A woman who celebrates sexy at sixty feels as sexy in a designer gown, sweaty exercise clothes, or naked. She usually has her own style that makes a powerful fashion statement that has nothing to do with the latest trends. She sets the trend.

Sexy at sixty is being comfortable in your skin knowing that it is your energy that is beautiful and engaging, not a size or an age. We are proud of our skin, our bodies, our age, and whatever size we happen to be. Sexy is a way of being. Sexy is a way of living. Sexy is a way of interacting. Sexy in your sixties sizzzls. I wouldn't want to be any other age. I wonder how much more powerful this energy can become in my seventies? Sexy at seventy-now that's a social contradiction. Look out! Sexy is being redefined!

Sexy, No Matter the Time and Life Circumstances
By Carol Wagner

The first time she appeared in my office door, she was apprehensive and later realized she was scared and emotionally distraught at what she had to do next. Even with the inevitable ahead of her, her hair with that unique white streak in the front, washing through a black background was perfectly coifed and sexy looking. She was dressed to the "nines" and dripping in diamonds and arrived chauffeured by John, in her very large, black Rolls Royce. The pure white interior of that car perfectly silhouetted her tiny and yet vibrant body.

Francie was going to have to place her so very beloved husband in a Skilled Nursing Facility and she was shopping for one. She had to have been in her mid 70's. She chose to trust us with the care of her beloved Mallory, who was pushing 80 at the time.

Mallory came to live with us and was elegant and debonair even in his state of poor health, Often I kidded with him that we would exchange his favorite dry Martini instead of the formula in the feeding bag (via a tube into his frail body) that hosted a menagerie of nutrients and medications that were helping him continue a quality of life as best as he could through the assistance of medical science. He could no longer swallow due to Parkinson's ugly manifestations even though he was mentally fine.

Oh the look in his eyes when Francie would arrive. He had been a confirmed bachelor and was heading to 50 years of age when he met her at a beach club. He was smitten by her confident and yet playful walk as she went to play tennis with some friends. (might have been that short tennis skirt and her attitude…) She was already a widow and thought another love was impossible and that it was over for her in the arena of romance.

Not at all so for Francie, these two played together and loved each other through sickness and health for over 30 years. The adventures they had are for another book! Those final years that I had the privilege of being witness to a part of their love story. This experience has put an impression on me of how and what a great love story and sexy woman can do to keep others inspired and live the gift of life to its fullest at every age.

Sprinting to Sixty
By Patricia Karen Gagic

In my 59 years of living there have been many wonderful adventures and collisions, roller coaster emotions and hurdles. The beauty of life is thrust into a delicate balance of the unknown with a seamless stream of inherent knowing. Being a Libran, my eyes see the candy before the floss, the golden arch in a rainbow before the separation of color and a frown is a smile turned upside down. As I reflect on my path, the journey has been one of immeasurable experiences that have created this terrific mind space for me to settle into. The heart was given many opportunities to reveal and be revealed.

Reflecting on what truly shaped my life, I would say it was meditation. Since 1972 I have been a practitioner and believe that was the shape shifter to a happy, content life. What I have come to appreciate and recognize is that there is an exotic kind of Spiritual sexiness and beauty that I have recognized in many people that seems to be outside of what would be considered cover girl beauty. Something inside of these people is raw and deeply appealing. There is an aura, an allure that seems almost angelic, a spiritual kind of beauty. You cannot see it nor is it tangible as in "she has beautiful hair"…but it exists. What makes someone who is basically considered average looking by normal standards appear to have such elusive beauty that magnetizes us to their presence? What is the quality that they possess that draws us so rapidly to them? I believe these people have open hearts, compassion and deep inner knowing of their own preciousness. Perhaps this wisdom that swells up improves our self-awareness and we learn to incorporate the Divine Goddess essence with our joyful nature. Something wonderful happens as we tap into and unlock our ego eyes and we push the refresh button and see beyond the skin, the shape of the nose or mouth. We are no longer distracted by what other people deem beautiful.

What makes the spectacular human appear beautiful, sexy, glamorous and desirable? Does the mind trick us into believing we are otherwise? Probably. All of the people who I have met that own the glow just radiate confidence as well as deadly, beaming smiles and lovely posture. Over time, our confidence matures as we evolve and tame the beast of negativity. With meditation and mindfulness practice we can permeate those dense walls and knock on the door of giving ourselves permission to enter, embrace and inhale our inner sexy beauty.

I love when I enter a room and someone taps me on the shoulder just with their glance. There is genuine warmth, an engaging and lingering hold of our attention. At that precise moment the gateway is open and the internal plethora of "the feel good feel" ignites within and as if by magic the skin blushes and a sparkle in the eye flashes and dances with the preciousness of life. That's powerful.

In meditation the heart and mind are purified into the joyful existence of being comforted by calmness and tranquility. Breathing changes and our actions and bodies awaken an inner courage. Something stimulates this courage and we are ignited to begin working on ourselves. We open up new levels of awareness to focus on what is within our grasp that perhaps we cannot see with our eyes. It is not a secret, it is accessible and we carry it with us at all times. It is our mind. Through meditation we can learn to de-clutter and calm our busy thoughts and relax our muscles and engage in the releasing of attachment to thoughts that bring us suffering. We enter into a loving, blissful, contented state of being that transcends us and our pores ooze with a gratefulness of being loved, loved by ourselves.

When I look in the mirror I see my physical body. My hair is thinning, my lips are thinning and my waist is not following suit. The bones and muscles remind me they have been well used. Years of racquetball, gymnastics, tennis, golf and running all brought grand pleasure at the time but a post mortem of pain. As I walk away from the mirror I realize that the mirror has no memory of me being there. It does not record my image because it cannot. Each time I reveal myself to the mirror it has no recollection of my previous visit.

But my mind recalls what I see and is quite capable of recording the changes. My first thought is what a phenomena this is. Can you imagine that you are in the greatest experience of the Universe…to have a physical body and a mind working together! We are given the delightful privilege of taking care of both with the ultimate gift which is to experience love. The mirror reflects our outer beauty, and if we are practicing meditation we earn inner peace that gently reflects itself back to us in the mirror and to all those who are in your presence. If we consider the mirror as a "teacher" we should allow ourselves to live in the moment just as the mirror only sees us in the moment of our appearance. There is only radiant light that snuffs out confusion and invites your soul to elevate to new heights.

Watching my body shift shape year after year, I allow my mind to absorb the good moments and release attachment from those that no longer serve me. While we watch our youthful bodies abandon us we are required to pay attention to our attitudes toward ourselves. If we have cultivated a good attitude towards our physical and mental concept of our femininity we will enjoy the essence of being who we have become. Only we can create and celebrate what we have created within. Imagine how new relationships will flourish based on a flawlessly executed love for one's own perfect self, no matter what the scars and flaws appear to be. We learn these "feel good" moments when we realize that our inherent beauty comes from a place very different than our physical presence. Taking the time to meditate daily, following a path towards respecting your beautiful physical body will engineer these qualities in you.

But what if by an act of shear randomness you are cut short from experiencing the same you that you have known and created.

What if your world is spun out of control by an accident that leaves you paralyzed, disfigured or blind? For those who have had such an experience you know exactly what that does to your confidence and your self-worth. We develop patterns of habit and engage ourselves in creating new thoughts about how we are perceived by others and whether or not we are attractive by the normal standards of beauty.

Scientists have researched the phenomena of beauty and have forensically determined that we are genetically engineered to define beauty by proportion as well as intelligence. What makes you feel beautiful is created within your own mind. I love to bring physics into everything…so I call this the Macro love bug. I start to appreciate myself cell by cell. It is the best way to start loving and appreciating yourself. Each cell connected together creating the synergy of just being. What a precious gift the human body and mind is. Over and over the body reproduces cells that replenish, and the magic reveals itself by our ability to heal. The bonuses follow with imagination, creativity and an inner glamour.

We often forget how much energy it takes to suffer via our own self-cherishing. It takes an incredible amount of energy to keep the mind busy and create words and actions that dismantle something that was created in perfection. What if you could cast this into a different light? What would happen if you visualized a scar or a flaw (that is only visible to you) as a beautiful source of pleasure? Sit quietly and imagine your scar separating into many tiny little pieces and ultimately it evaporates… When we open our eyes again to see what really exists we will find the beauty of having re-created it from its macro-state of ugly to its perfect vibration of beauty. Each time you look at it you will be a reminded of its perfection and as a whole entity it becomes a familiar beautiful part of you. You will begin to embrace its beauty and find it is no longer a source of suffering.

This is what happened to me. Four moments in time that brought a death, a birth, a head on collision and surgery, three accidents over three decades leaving sexy out the door and off the floor. Somehow I had equipped myself with great ideas about who I thought I was. But ideas are just that and when it came time to facing the battle ground of life I was met by a formidable opponent, my ego. You know, as we get on with life, meet our karma partners, develop karma chats and blunder through the landscape of the mind things seem to get tougher and more challenging. What never left me was the "idea" of who I was and that became the agent of change for me. The Warrior Woman kicked in with the attitude that no matter what I look like, my heart and mind are in the right place. I can serve others and love the very same way.

Feeling sorry for oneself is ego driven. In the bigger picture, whatever you believe is made up of your own perception and vision of what your mind has created about yourself. People will either like you with or without your flaws and the results are either permission granted or denied. If there is a puzzle piece to sexy with no boundaries it lies in awakening your beautiful mind to loving all of you. No matter what your age is, if you take the time to cultivate the source of light within you will remain sexy and sprinting! You are simply being. Take the challenge and maybe sprinting to ninety will only be the first plateau!!!

Chapter 4

Confession of the Sexy Spat

"Scars are merely permanent reminder of temporary feeling."
—Jimmy Buffet

"Beauty can come from the strangest of places,
even the most disgusting of places"
—Alexander McQueen

"We're the song inside the tune. Full of beautiful mistakes…"
—Christina Aguilera's song "Beautiful"

I love antiques! People come to my house and always tell me that my house looks like a museum. Indeed, I like to collect paintings, posters, sculptures, glasses, crystals, ceramics…I like to watch "Antique Roadshow" from PBS. I like to be educated by all those appraisers "What is it worth?" "What is not?" "Why is it worth so much?" "What is the history?" One thing that I learned from this show is that there is something called "conversational value". Conversational value is when you display that interesting object in your living room, it will raise the curiosity and the conversations begin.

My boyfriend had a coaching client came to our house one day for coaching. Before he left, I showed him around. When he saw that I have many antiques, he told me that his wife likes antiques too. I showed him the two paintings that are hanging in my living room which are painted by my brother. Then he went on to describe to me that he has a tapestry hanging in his living room which shows medieval knights and horses. He went on to describe how beautiful the tapestry is then I remember a similar tapestry that was hanging in my guest bed room. I went off to grab the tapestry and showed it to him. I asked, "Is it this one?" His eyes almost popped out of his head when he saw the tapestry! We have the exact, same tapestry! The only difference is that I have mine hung on a metal rod while his is in a glass and wooden frame. We had so much fun talking about how we both appreciated that particular tapestry. Ah ha! That is conversational value!

Then one day, I discovered conversational value from someone's face! I knew this speaker for a few years. But I had never noticed that he has a scar on his face. At one point while we were talking, I suddenly saw his scar in his left cheek! So I asked him where it came from. To my surprise, he told me that it is his battle with skin cancer. Having worked as life guard, the long term exposure under the sun was dangerous. There is always a story behind every scar; it's an ice breaker for a conversation. Because of "his" conversational value, our friendship got closer.

The mass media extensively promote flawless beauty, especially in Hollywood. I am glad to hear from some of the famous celebrities who stand tall and talk openly how much they believe that their imperfection represents who they are, it's a trade mark for them. Whether the imperfection is from birth, or formed after an accident, when one can manage to see beyond that visual imperfection, one can take that as a signature trait and turn into her/his beauty mark. It is the blueprint of one's life.

Michael Strahan, the former NFL pro and co-host of "Live! With Kelly and Michael" has a gap in his front teeth. In his twenties, he had the pressure of being perfect while playing with the greats in the athletic world. He came close to getting the gap in his teeth closed, but in the end, he pulled the plug, and decided that he was going to embrace his imperfection.

He made a conscious effort to accept who he is. "I am not perfect. I don't want to try to be perfect". His fans think that it is his trademark and it adds character and sexiness to his already beautiful body. Nowadays, with his great sense of humor, he can even joke that his children might not be able to recognize him if he ever fixes the gap.

There are many more celebrities through the years who have proved to us that the tiny flaw doesn't determine one's success even in a world that is based very much on appearance. Brigitte Bardot (The French bombshell in the 50's), Lauren Hutton (The super model) and Madonna all represent huge success in different eras despite their iconic gap teeth smile. Instead of discouraging their sexiness, their imperfect gap teeth made them sexier.

Despite the 7 inch scar on her right arm which was the result of a car accident when she was 14 years old, the famous model and host of the US reality television program "Top Chef", Padma Lakshmi reveals that her permanent scar became her most favorite part of her body. Well, it was not an instant "love at first sight"; it took her a few years to overcome her worry that she cannot be successful in her modeling career. She even went through some painful treatments to lighten the scar.

Today, the confident Padma has no problem of showing it off; in fact, she wears it like a trophy, like a medal on a soldier's jacket. She finally realized that it is the blueprint of her life–emotionally or physically. It reminds her that she can survive in tough circumstances. Her fans believe that the scar adds an alluring attractiveness to her already sensual beauty.

She even said that if there is a doctor who could wave a magic wand and remove it from her arm, she is not sure if she wants to remove it. She sets a great example to us that even in Hollywood, one doesn't need to be perfect to be successful. A slight flaw actually adds certain sexiness to oneself.

In fact, even the spokeswoman Paula Karaiskos from the Storm modeling agency (the one that discovered Kate Moss) confirms that their clients were actually looking for individuals who carry *"a little individual imperfection"*. Instead of a girl being boringly beautiful, quirky flaws such as freckles, less-than-perfect noses, being short actually lends authority and adds attractiveness in one self. They say that physical traits look more mysterious and interesting. The idea is to keep a little individual imperfection.

I also heard about battle wounds as being highly praised. Indeed! There is a song "War Wounds", the lyrics say, "Check my war wounds (uggggh) My war wounds (ugggh) Every soldier got a story to tell."

Scars are the medals on a soldier's jacket. They are the memories of their heroic life. They are the history to be remembered, to be recognized, to be acknowledged. The lasting scars were the evidence of what it took to be who they are.

Whether your scar is the memories from the battle of life or death, or from a disease, or from an accident, they all are exciting tales to be told and the beginning of a conversation.

Beyond the conversational value of the imperfection, scars give you character. No two scars are alike. They are unique, just like tattoos, but they are naturally formed, instead of carefully inked into your skin.

Yes, I have a major scar under my tummy due to my C-section. That is the mark of Life-when I gave birth to my two beautiful and healthy sons. To me, no matter how horrible my experience was in the delivery of my babies, these scars only left me the best memories of what I did in this world.

Most people dislike scars, it is a sign of imperfection. But in the world of Body Art, there are African tribes who celebrate the stage of maturity by marking scars on their faces, or to their bodies. They believe that is the implementation of adding sexual attraction to oneself. Of course, this is a bi-product of the diverse cultural background. People are interested in finding out what caused Seal's facial scars. How could he win Heidi Klum over?

In fact, the scar in Seal's face is so perfectly lay out that I almost thought that they are the result from the Body Art. On the contrary, he actually suffers from discoid lupus erythematosus which left him the scars on his face. Fortunately, somebody like Heidi Klum can see through the physical appearance and deeply attracted by his talent, his inner soul and his eternal beauty.

Scars are a part of who you are, there are always stories behind them. If we can look beyond the surface of what is normal and start to discover the inner layer, the history of the imperfection, we will notice the beauty.

It is encouraging to see Michael Weiss who suffers from many health issues, experienced many different surgeries, yet his scars were appreciated by his girlfriend. She thinks that they are sexy. Michael not being discouraged by his health issues and the permanent scars on his body, he went so far as to create a YouTube video, with the purpose of contributing to the charitable *"Scars-R-Sexy"* campaign. I love to see individuals turn their misfortune into an arc of a rainbow where people can climb up and reach the highness.

The Scars of Time Are Just Lines
By Amy Regenstreif

I have had stage 4 retroperitoneal leiomyosarcoma for 10 years. I have had this very rare cancer since 2001. I was only 44 years young and quite healthy when I was first diagnosed. In these 12 years I have had 12 abdominal surgeries, 4 tries at chemo therapy, and I have been bald twice. I have had 2 stomach ports, 2 chest ports, a pic line and much other stuff. My face is a happy one however I have a face on my body as well :), due to so many scars. I call them the lines of time that define the strength and power in me. They are not scars, which have a negative connotation.

I am alive because of those scars.

I have no female parts, no gall bladder and less of every digestive part that you can think of. I have redefined my body image so that I can live with myself many times over these years. Can you imagine the thoughts of sensuality, lingerie, and sex that might go through my mind? Every person going through an illness and/or a disability is different. This is how I have learned to help myself and love myself all of these years.

In the early years of my diagnosis I did not think much about loving my body, dating, sex, etc. I had just gotten divorced and had twin daughters 11 years old at the time, and my life revolved around them. I thought that I had plenty of time to think about all of those other life issues. I was enjoying a time of remission. I even thought that I was "cured".

In mid 2005 I was standing in my office and a man walked in to come to my seminar. At the end of the event he asked me out for coffee. I said yes and thought…good for business and he is cute! We had coffee for 4 hours. To make a long story short, this was the beginning of an 8 year crazy, fun, loving relationship, with too many life ups and downs, and I had cancer throughout much of these years so I cannot talk about my body without discussing him a little bit. He helped me so much.

For you ladies…funny…we discovered that our age difference was 15 years! Me older! Do the math :). He was so excited that I had no female parts! No worries on birth control at all…that is a very freeing feeling believe it or not!

Time passed and we were having a blast until that moment in 2007 when remission was over. My cancer came back with a vengence. Chemos, surgery, etc, etc.

Looking naked in the mirror I saw a middle aged woman with no hair, not just bald, no hair anywhere. I had a chest port, a permanent lump in my chest where people put tubes and take blood. How sexy was this? How sensual was this? How do I wrap myself around this with a boyfriend 15 years younger than me?

My boyfriend shaved my head with his electric razor and told me every day to this day how beautiful I was. He bought me lingerie that covered my lines and we had sex with my chest port in for years. With his help, the help of others and my own power to make decisions that were in my best interest no matter what, I just kept moving forward.

We have since separated. The threat of my possible early demise was just too much for him. I have made peace with everything. It was a lot of work however I did it. I do not want you to think this journey has been easy. I have had my moments like everyone else.

You must accept certain things. Your body will age, perhaps before its time. Let your ideas of sensuality mature and change with you. Do not let your illness or disability define you. Learn to love yourself whether you age with a significant other or not. You may age just with your friends.

I have learned to love my body just the way it is because I am alive and it is working! One day it might not and I will be gone. I like it here!

I swim, play the conga drum, and walk miles. I eat healthy and I laugh a lot. I want to have fun with fabulous people.

The key to accepting your body is the same as in life itself...to be able to accept change, adapt, seek positive support and keep moving forward! Use the parts that work. Always use the parts that work.

I am 56 years young now. I am trying to develop muscle and gain some weight at this time. It's not because I do not like the way I look. It is because I need some extra pounds in case this crazy disease returns! My frame of reference is a bit different! Love and Joy to you.

Sexy is the anticipation
By Siouxsie

I didn't really know what sexy was until I met him. He changed my perception of what sexy could be. I was working as a photographer for the music industry, travelling around the country with bands, promoting the music business. In 2002 I started photographing nudes. My nudes were displayed in galleries on both coasts and appeared in print as well. They were beautiful, classic and sensual-but they were not sexy-nor did I intend for them to be.

As much as I enjoyed working with the play of light on skin, after a while I realized that I needed to breakthrough to another level with my art. I had reached the point of "Yeah, and so?" It was time to explore something new, but I didn't know what.

That's when it happened. I heard about a pop-up erotic art gallery in the Valley so a friend and I headed over and blended in with a group that was clearly on the guest list. We were amazed by the number of artists whose work was on display. Work that one would not normally see in the San Fernando Valley!

I was drawn to some exotic and beautiful images of Asian bondage photography. I was captivated by the ethereal lighting, the delicate, dancer-like poses of the models, and the exquisite beauty of the Japanese decorative rope knots and the rich, vibrant colors of the prints.

I spoke to the photographer and told him that I was looking for a new direction in my art and that his images spoke to me. He suggested that I should figure out what is sexy to me and photograph that. He also warned that I must understand my subject before I attempt to photograph it and he offered to introduce me to some of the inhabitants of his world.

I accompanied him to a dungeon. It was a dimly lit place where people were dressed in all sorts of costuming—or not. Scenes were being played out in various locations throughout the property. Here were strange pieces of furniture and odd contraptions that put ones imagination in overdrive. Some people stood in groups and chatted against a background of chilling audio effects that seemed right out of a haunted castle or horror film. I was particularly sensitive to the sounds and had to depart before too long.

Later, I had the opportunity to meet some of the players under less dramatic circumstances and attended classes on knife-play, rope-tying and flogging. There was a lot of talk about safety and responsibility and taking care of each other.

I began to see the sexiness in the mutual trust and in the exchange of power. One person gives permission to the other to take total control, with the understanding that with control comes responsibility. The willingness to give up power and control and let someone else be in charge may appear to be a weakness but actually requires a special kind of strength and a tremendous amount of trust. Being the recipient of that trust, that power, that control, requires another kind of strength because it means being responsible for the safety and well-being of someone else. There is a level of passion in these relationships that is noticeably present but not easily expressed. Both parties are in agreement that they are participating by choice and can end it at will.

At one point, a knife vendor approached me about photographing some of his product. He had some beautiful custom knives that we would bring to my studio along with some models. It was great to have such interesting subjects to light and photograph. The models were very comfortable around the knives and skilled in handling them. I thought about what the photographer had said to me about figuring out what was sexy to me and I realized that interaction of the models with the knives was sexy. The way they would hold the blade lightly against the skin, with a slight intake of breath now and then, there was such an intimacy around the trust they shared. They were very careful and attentive towards each other, and very focused. They had to be.

There was something very special and intriguing happening here. As I looked through my camera lens, I looked not only with my eyes, but also with my heart. Why was this sexy to me? I think it was the edginess of the danger. Sexy-scary. I like to capture moments. When I capture a unique moment in a photograph, it is a small victory. The best moment to capture is the moment just before something happens. It is not an easy thing to capture. You lie in wait for it and concentrate and anticipate. Time slows down when you anticipate. You experience the breath between the seconds.

That time spent in anticipation is sexy to me. When you don't know what is going to happen next and you are waiting. If you close your eyes and there is someone nearby and you know they will soon touch you but you don't know where or when, that is sexy. With your eyes closed you become more aware of the sounds, the smells, your senses are heightened. Now, what if you are blindfolded and your arms are restrained so that you have no choice but to be still and listen and feel and wait for something to happen. That breathless anticipation of a touch, or a kiss, or ???? Very sexy!

It is that anticipation that I love to capture in an image as much as I love to experience it myself. Giving in to vulnerability and allowing the scariness and the uncertainty while wondering what is going to happen and trusting that whatever comes will be okay can be a very sexy experience. Come to think of it, that sounds like my everyday life. Funny…In one part of my life, that is called sexy, and in another part of my life I call it stress. The next time I think I am feeling stressed, I will have to remind myself that I'm actually feeling sexy!

It was through my art that I discovered my sexy. It is a wonderful thing!

It's an everyday Deal!
By Mayra Abruzzo

I was not even 30 when I was told by my doctor that I had breast cancer. Coming from a family that had absolutely no history of cancer was really a shock to me. Instead of asking GOD "Why me?" I ask myself, "How am I going to deal with it?"

On one hand, I have to deal with my dramatic physical change; on the other hand, I had to pretend in front of my husband and my two young sons that there was nothing ever happened to me. One part of me was so vulnerable while the other part of me told me that I have to stay strong. I didn't want them to feel sorry for me; I didn't want them to go through everyday life with the back of their head telling them that I am a sick person.

As much as I tried to act normal, things appeared abnormal when I realized that my hair was falling out uncontrollably. I started to find big chunks of hair scattered everywhere in the house. In order to not be so dramatic, I decided to shave it all off. After all, there are lots of beautiful wigs out there; or I can wrap a colorful scarf around my bald head; or wear a trendy hat…the choices are unlimited! Next thing I know, I lost my eyelashes and my eye blows…literally every strand of my body hair was gone.

As much as I was told that it is normal to lose my body hair; as much as I was told that I should accept that I may look "sick", I had no intention to look or act like a cancer patient and feel sorry for myself; or have anyone feel sorry for me. I decided that I am going to look good! I am going to create my *"New Normal"*. I went to MAX in the mall and explained to the makeup expert what was I going through. I asked her to teach me how to draw my eye brows, how to custom construct a makeup that has no body hair, moreover, my skin tone has gone from pale to even more pale. I felt like I was painting on a pale white canvas. I still want to look beautiful in front of my husband and my kids. So much so that sometimes, I actually forgot that I had cancer!

But it came to remind me when I experienced going through all the changes that were supposed to be happening twenty years later in my life. I went through menopause, the side effect of the chemo treatment caused my weight to go up, my nails start to be crapped up...there were definitely abnormalities that I had to deal with in daily life. All those little things became an everyday ordeal for me.

I know that many women take photos during the whole process of the chemo. They want to keep a record of how things changed. For whatever reason, I did not take any pictures of myself during that time. I did not want my children to look at the picture and recall when their mother was sick. I did not want to bring forward any unpleasant memories. I did not want to whine and carry my grief every day. I decided to put it in the back of my head and enjoy today and just look forward.

Instead of recording what was changing in me during my battle with cancer, I decided to share my wisdom with those who also have cancer, or those who have cancer in the family. I wrote a book about how things changed and how to adopt the "New Normal". What is the alternative? By doing that I felt good and up-lifted.

How did my outfits change? There wasn't a major change in my fashion wardrobe, but I have to admit that I had put away my sexy lingerie. Either did I felt not in the mood; or I knew that it didn't fit me anymore. Or whatever reason it was, I knew that it wasn't my priority.

My journey through the Chemo treatment was like riding a roller coaster. There were times when I became emotionally very vulnerable. When it happened, I could not control all the negative thoughts that went through my head. I know that the negative thoughts could kill me, not the cancer. So I decided to really take care of my health so I can straighten things up. I realized that I needed to stay calm, keep peace within myself. I think my martial arts background did help me with discipline in many aspects of my life.

I started to learn to meditate. And I listed all the positive things about myself and I placed it on my desk where it crossed my eyes many times in a day. I read them out loud so that I could hear my own voice. This was the confirmation of my self-love manifestation.

I also tried to watch TV programs that were up-lifting, positive messages; or just silly jokes…whatever could make me laugh. I remembered vividly one day while I was asking the question "Why me?" again, I suddenly felt that it was so nice to be me yesterday. Why on earth wasn't I enjoying what I had before? Maybe it was that "my yesterday" didn't fore-see what is "my today"! That was the moment when I understood why people said "enjoy the present"! So I decided not to imagine what is going to happen after I pass away (that my husband is going to marry someone else, and my kids are going to have a step mother…) I decided to live for the moment.

I remember one Christmas, my husband told me that both of us were invited to his company's Christmas party and asked if I would like to go with him. "YES!" I said cheerfully and he reacted a little surprised. In fact, I decided to enjoy every moment of my precious life. I even bought a blond racy wig for the party! I think I was so bold because I realized that there was nothing to lose. Why do I have to hold myself back? On the party day, I had my full make-up and I wore a pretty dress that shows my beautiful cleavage. People told me that I looked like a bimbo. Thank GOD for the magical lingerie! I did enjoy that night very much!

Remember when I told you that I had put away my sexy lingerie? It was hard! Since my whole life, I enjoyed my sexy lingerie. I felt that I was sexy, powerful, confident and attractive. I was always a Victoria's Secret kind of girl. After my marriage, my sexy lingerie did magical work for our relationship. So parting with my sexy lingerie was very hard for me. Well, not forever! After I finished my Chemo, I slowly grew back my hair. I started to want to be attractive not only outside the bedroom, but also inside my bedroom. I never would have thought that it took me so much courage to enter again the Victoria's Secret store. The courage is to forget that I do not have a complete body anymore. After the Chemo and the radiation, I now have a partially desensitized breast. It is hard for me to pass that boundary of what I can do and what I cannot do.

Yes, I wear sexy lingerie again! It actually helps me with my new breasts. I still look good and most importantly, I feel sexy and confident again. I know that it will never be the same, with the huge scare right underneath my breast, but I also know that I have to live with what I have, not what I had. I could have been a lot worse! Having a supportive love is the core of fighting any battle. Whether it is the love from your loved one, or the love from yourself. Life is a blessing!

Chapter 5

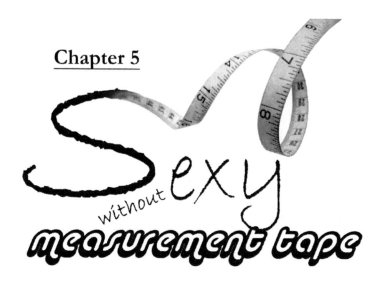

Sexy *without* measurement tape

"There is more to sex appeal than just measurements. I don't need a bedroom to prove my womanliness. I can convey just as much sex appeal, picking apples off a tree or standing in the rain."
—Audrey Hepburn

"If you think you are too small to make a difference, try sleeping with a mosquito."
—Dalai Lama

"I finally realized that being grateful to my body was key to giving more love to myself."
—Oprah Winfrey

"Women of every age and size really just want to look sexy, while retaining their power and dignity."
—L'Wren Scott

This is me!

If you know me personally, you should know that I am petite-five feet tall; weighing 100 pounds. I don't have much of a bust and my body is rectangular shape (in fashion industry term…that means that my bust, waist and hips are almost the same size). This is me!

At this point, I have to introduce you to my Vietnamese friend, Natalie. She is the one who is responsible for my beautiful nails that everyone admires.

Natalie has huge breasts, 34DD+, and her butt is well rounded, a perfect hour-glass figure. But she told me that it wasn't her real body. She told me that her real bust size was 34A; then she had a breast implant, she turned into a 34C+. She enjoyed it for some time, and then she decided that it wasn't big enough for her. She decided to up-grade herself to a 34DD+. For her butt, she doesn't wear those padded panties every day; but when she does, she makes sure to tell me and has me admire her up-lifted and well rounded behind!

Natalie likes to check me out every day. She likes to look at me from head to toe and admire how I put myself together. After all, having style is a whole package!

One day, while she was doing my French manicure, she said to me, "Hidi, you look young, beautiful, you dress so nice every day and you have money; all you need is to have a pair of big boobs! If you have big boobs, ohhhhhhhh, you will look so HOT!" In the meantime, she was making a face as if she got burnt by how hot I will be. She went on, "All the men will be so crazy for you!" I was frozen for 2 seconds, then I smiled and said to her, "No, I am fine as I am. I don't need to have big tits. You see, many models don't have much boobs. I don't think Kate Moss has much bigger tits than mine. I don't need to have the tits like Dolly Parton to cross the finishing line in a marathon. At least I am proportional! Actually, having a flatter chest does hang clothes better!

Of course, coming from Natalie, I can understand why she wants me to have a breast implant. She just wants me to look beautiful and sexy. But I am so happy that I know I don't need that to prove my sex appeal. As Audrey Hepburn once said, "There is more to sex appeal than just measurements. I don't need a bedroom to prove my womanliness. I can convey just as much sex appeal, picking apples off a tree or standing in the rain." Being a lingerie designer, I always know how to dress to accentuate my sexiness. It is in the choice of my outfit. It is how I put them together, it is a whole package. It is an art!

I know how important your first impression is, as the Italian fashion power house, Miuccia Prada once said, "Fashion is an instant language". Indeed, before you open your mouth, the way you dress already speaks for you. No wonder I saw a billboard from Ann Taylor's hiring event. They said "Dress to impress" before "Bring your resume"! Make your first impression is of utmost importance in any situation. Whether you are going for a blind-date; having a job interview; finally meeting your online customer off-line…are you making an impression? Or are you breaking an impression? Make sure that you put as much effort into your look as into your resume or presentation. Dressing up-to-date will give you an air of awareness, open-minded, stay with the current technology, creative, respected–you can convey your charm effectively. Otherwise, if your outfit is out-dated, or even worse, sloppy, you will then be seen as conservative, narrow minded and not innovated-it might even decrease your power of speech! A good first impression will make you stay on the list, otherwise, you will be checked off the list.

Having said that your first impression is important; but who will bear a pretty woman with no brains, no personality, or no inner quality? I know that when I pass that first impression in a stranger's eye, it is my inner beauty that they are searching for. It is the positive attitude with which I present myself. It is my confidence to speak my mind. It is my sense of humor that I know I can make fun of myself and even make others laugh. It is the power within my creative mind. It is my determination to not give up and to pursue what I promised myself. It is my authenticity towards my friends and family. It is my gratitude towards those who have planted their seeds in me. It is my wisdom that I share with others…and this is me.

Everybody wants to be a NFL player but nobody wants to practice. There are so many people who want to be someone else; or to have someone's body. *The grass is always greener on the other side of the fence.* Yes, if being overweight is your concern, do something about it! Get on a regular diet and stick with it. Exercise to lose fat and calories. Celebrities don't just have a fabulous body and flawless skin. They exercise a lot and have a restricted diet to stay in shape. If even the celebrities have to do that, you think you can achieve that without any actions? Set your goal and work on it instead of just whining about how overweight you are.

At the same time, having a positive opinion of yourself is very important. If you don't love yourself, you can never fully love someone in the way they deserve you. Poor self-image leads to no sexiness, only a rich belief in oneself is attractive to others.

How much you value yourself depends on your confidence level. In Chapter One, I talked about how confidence makes up a majority part of being sexy. So people ask me, "How do I gain more confidence?" The answer to this question is really simple. Confidence doesn't come all of a sudden by the boat load. It is an accumulation of "pieces of confidence". When we add all those pieces of confidences together, it becomes the amount of confidence that we carry within ourselves. We receive confidence when we are complimented by others; your boss gives you a pat on the back to say you did a good job. Or your husband compliments you on the meal that you cooked. Or your friend tells you how great you look in that dress. Or receiving applause after you gave your speech.

We all know that all these little compliments given by the others boost up our confidence. But most of us forget to acknowledge ourselves when it comes to our achievements. I believe that not only should you acknowledge other people, but acknowledge yourself too. Pat yourself on the back when you achieve something. But I am not here to encourage you to become egotistic! There is a fine line there.

I know that some successful people will give a gift to themselves or someone they love for every significant achievement. After all, giving can be as happy as receiving. Just like Barbara Corcoran, the female shark in the popular TV show "Shark Tank". When she made her first million dollars, she bought a brand new car for each of her parents! The sense of achievement will boost your confidence. All of a sudden, you feel like you are 10 feet tall, you walk with your shoulders back, your chin up-the feeling of accomplishment is very rewarding. Of course, we don't need to make a million in order to show acknowledgement to ourselves, or someone we love, even a little gesture will help.

We tend to overlook our own effort on anything, we take it for granted. So next time, when you finish a job, give yourself credit. For me, I put all my achievements in my resume. When I did a seminar, a workshop, an intensive, wrote a book, being a judge at a Fashion school, having my designs in a runway show, being the feature of a fashion magazine...I put them down in my resume. By reading my resume, I have that sense of achievement. It is indeed a very wonderful reward to me. Of course, sometimes, I buy myself a piece of jewelry, or a pair of shoes, or get myself a ticket to the concert that I have been longing for.

What will you do to reward your next achievement?

Relaxing Into My Sexy
By Amy Cheyl

"Amy, I'm giving your yoga class to someone else."

"What?!? What do you mean? This makes no sense. I've built a following, which usually means the opposite. What's really going on, Barbara*? I need to know the truth."

"It's not that I don't adore you, it's just that, quite frankly, you are too 'goddessy' and sexy. We are looking for a more militant instructor. You know, like Jane. Maybe you can take her class and learn her style, and then I can keep you on the sub list."

I took a deep breath to steady myself and find the right words when suddenly, I was shot back in time-feeling horrible shame when I was 7 years old, prancing around the house in my birthday suit, hearing my mom yell, "Amy, put your shirt on. You're going to embarrass your dad!"

Floods of memories overwhelmed me—images and feelings connected to all the times I was told I was "too much," or to "try to be this way or that way so others won't be uncomfortable around you." And then the many times when I felt good in what I was wearing and someone said, "You are wearing THAT?!? Don't you think it's a little too...well, you know...revealing?"

Then there was the devastating phone call that banned me from my favorite yoga class because the instructor's wife felt threatened by my presence, "Amy, I can't have you take my class anymore. Sorry."

With every one of these memories, feelings of shame intensified-not shame around what I did, but shame around who I was. Suddenly, I felt angry and sick.

Again?!? What am I going to do this time? Looking at Barbara, I continued searching for words as I flashed on the faces of every mean girl from grade school, through my twenties in the workplace, and remembered the pain of dimming myself down to fit in, trying to not stand out or upset others with my naturally intense sensuality. I remembered the disgust of living in my body after gaining over 80 pounds by 14 years old to try to hide any semblance of sexy, as even I had somehow become uncomfortable with all the attention, and how it seemed to make others upset.

I was no longer the carefree spirit that ran through the house happy to be naked and free. Even after I lost the weight at 15 years old, I was uncomfortable in my own skin and didn't know how to make it safe for me to be myself again.

Eventually, the repeated message that the mere essence of who I am-a playful, free-spirited, sensual, alive, and radiant being-was not okay, took its toll on me. As people and situations in my life reinforced my insecurities and fears, my self-worth disappeared and deeply affected my career path and my relationships.

So concerned about what others would think of me, and whether I'd be accepted and liked, I gave up my dream of being on stage-the one place that brought me the greatest joy-after noticing that I always seemed to be the one stirring up trouble with my presence.

Whether it was the thoughtless words of my peers, the moms who got angry that their daughters didn't get the lead part, or the trainers who tried to blacklist me and run me out of fitness clubs, I got tired of being a target. It was emotionally upsetting and exhausting. I couldn't believe how people would go out of their way to sabotage my efforts to be happy, to do what I love…to be me.

How could this happen again? I thought I moved past this. Why are people afraid of my sensuality, and why do I keep dimming myself to fit in?

I took another deep breath. The energy in me was finally refusing to be suppressed and put aside.

Screw that! I'm not going to play that game anymore!

I was done being too much for other peoples' comfort levels. That was not "my stuff," and I was done owning it.

What if I'm not meant to "fit in" and contort myself to be something I'm not? Perhaps it's time that I relax into my own sensual self and stop compromising my essence for the sake of others.

"Thank you for your honesty, Barbara." Even though I felt it was totally unjustified, and my insides were on fire with indignation, I forced a smile and walked away, not just from the job, but from the game—the game of dimming my sexy to fit in.

Little did I know, I was walking into the inspiration for my future work as a mentor who helps women understand and own their magnetic power rather than dim or run away from it.

————

A few weeks passed, and the fire inside me grew.

I'll never find a place of work where they'll accept my sensuality. Seriously, they're the ones that need to deal with their fear and embrace their own sexy selves.

As that thought crossed my mind, I experienced clarity about my life like never before.

What if this is why I'm here? To embrace my divine sexy self, and to help other women do the same? Every woman has a right to feel the joy and liberation of being sexy, accepting the totality of herself, and experiencing playfulness and pleasure. It's who we are, and it cannot be suppressed without dangerous consequences.

I reflected on the years I'd dragged around 80 extra pounds in an effort to hide, and then I saw the faces of the men I'd invited into my life.

Yes, dangerous and heartbreaking consequences.

I shook my head, remembering how my lack of self-worth had me either attract men that were no good for me, or use my sensuality to numb the pain of heartbreak by seducing or even controlling them. Yes, at one point, I used my sensuality as a weapon to get back at men, and to protect me from more pain. With no idea how to wield my sensual power, or what healthy boundaries were, I fell victim to the drug of lust; and after a few years of giving my power away, I found myself desperate for change.

The day I witnessed myself on the floor, begging an ex-convict to take me back when every rational part of me screamed, "No," I finally saw my life clearly. Curled up in a ball, sobbing on the floor, I felt as if I was back in my 7-year-old self, crying in terror and feeling powerless to deal with the rage and emotional abuse I experienced as a little girl. When the flashback subsided, I could see how I'd somehow been recreating the chaos and emotional pain in my relationships because it was all I'd ever known with men. How could I possibly create a healthy, loving relationship with a man when the little girl in me was terrified that he would turn into my father the minute I let my guard down?

That was the day I decided to do whatever it took to heal my childhood pain so that I could feel safe with men...and safe with myself again.

My God-given gift, my sensuality, had become something I not only judged and felt afraid of, and something that had elicited judgment from others and isolated me, but it was now causing me to self-destruct and take others with me.

Maybe I can save other women from this type of pain by embracing my own sexy and creating a safe space for other women to do that as well...

The inspiration began to flow, and I created a new workout system that was all about feeling sexy and playful again, and experiencing that this is how we free ourselves. I got so excited about the possibility of seeing women really fall in love with their true sexy, carefree selves and their bodies, and take that love back into their relationships with self and others, and into their career. The fact that I was going to create a space where I could safely be myself was icing on the cake.

Finally seeing that a women's self-confidence comes from her ability to love, not judge, all aspects of herself-especially her sensual, playful sexy self-I began teaching my "Sensual Diva" classes.

As I shared the opportunity, I heard, "Oh, that's not me; I'm not sensual. I wish I could be though," or "Oh, I can't move like that," and it broke my heart to hear how many women are disconnected from their essence.

It wasn't long before I noticed my passion for teaching fitness being overshadowed by a burning desire to move deeper into mentorship. There was obviously so much more to helping women feel safe in their sexy, and I felt called to help.

I loved the counseling work, but soon found myself "hiding" again, running away from the stage *again* by spending all of my time with one-on-one clients when I'd been inspired to take my message to bigger audiences. I knew that I was not fully living my full divine purpose.

This realization brought about a whole new unfolding of fears, revealing wounds that I knew I needed to dive into. Speaking about my journey would expose me in a whole new way, and I had to make sure I was ready. There would be no choreography, sweat, or music to hide behind.

Am I ready to put that stake in the ground and fully reclaim myself, stepping out full-force, taking on this controversial and completely misunderstood conversation, and being truly visible and transparent at that?

I panicked, as the thought of being a target again became a possibility again.

Do I have the strength to handle it? My answer came from deep within. *Yes! The thought of not following this path, when every experience of my life journey points in the direction of molding me for this message, makes me depressed. But there's work to do...*

I felt like I was dying inside. I was determined to figure this out, and I knew the only way out was *through*.

Five years later, I'm so glad I decided to dive into the deep end of healing old wounds and fully embracing my sensual, playful self. I've learned how to enjoy and wield this energy, heal my relationship with my father, create and enforce healthy boundaries with men, and see other women, not through the lens of judgment and fear, but through eyes of love and compassion. I've come to truly believe that until we, as women, fully love ourselves, and acknowledge, own, and feel safe in our sexiness, we will forever be irritated by and jealous of the women who do. In a society that cultivates competition, women are the ones who could most naturally and easily model collaboration, but not if we are constantly judging each other and ourselves.

It's time, Ladies, for us to relax into our sexy selves. As we fully embrace our sensuality, our bodies, our relationships, our careers, and our world will become a safer, more joyful place for all of us to live.

*Names have been changed to respect the privacy of others.

What Really Matters
By Jack M. Zufelt

My relationship with Marci, my wife of 37 years started as a blind date. Her roommate told me she was dating someone who was not good for her and asked me to see if I could do something about that. Even back then at age 25 I had a reputation for helping others so I said I would "reach out to her and see what I could do to change her situation." I had no idea what she looked like and I didn't care. I was on a mission to "save a soul" or "help a lady in distress".

It took me 6 weeks to get a "date" with her because she was a Systems Engineer for IBM and traveled a lot. I shall never forget what happened the night I went to pick her up! When she opened the door of her apartment and I saw her for the first time…I have to confess…my motive for going out with her to "help" her instantly changed! She was stunning! Her face is all I saw and all that I remember. Not her body, not her shape, not anything to do with sexiness but her face…with her hair in a bun on the back of her head. I was suddenly personally interested in her as a woman not a project or someone to save.

Our date was at a Japanese restaurant where you sit on the floor in a booth with sliding paper doors that closed off to make it private. We sat low on the floor with the table between us at about mid-chest level. I could only see her face so my interest in her was still from the neck up not the neck down. We sat in that booth for six hours! It only took an hour to eat and then we just drank water the rest of the time!

During that very long "dinner date", something happened that I have never before experienced! It was pure magic! At the beginning of our conversation she asked me to tell her about myself. I was afraid to do that because of my past. It was not good. Before I accepted Jesus Christ as my Savior I was not a good man. I was a rebellious soul… the kind of son every mother hopes they don't get. I had been on the wrong side of the law, I had been married and divorced by the time I was 22. I had two children from that marriage. I did NOT want to tell all that ugly history.

I was prompted from above to "be without guile" and speak the truth. So I did. Fearfully, I said, "I don't want to tell you about my past." Her response was, "Why not?" Again prompted from a source beyond me, I spoke truth again. I said, "Because I am afraid that if I tell you about my past you won't like me." Even though, because of my desire to follow Christ and do my best to be like Him I was afraid she would not understand or believe that. I had changed and had become a new man, a good man with a commitment to do and be good but I had a belief that she would not like me if she only knew all about my past.

She said, "I doubt that but try me." So I told her everything. I held nothing back. I told her all the ugly about my youth, my marriage and two children and what kind of man I was until I was 24. After doing that I then fearfully asked, "So how does that information make you feel about me now?" What happened next opened my eyes to a truth that is wonderful.

She said, "I don't like you less. I like you more!" What?!?!? I was astonished! Stunned, I asked her, "Why do you like me *more* after hearing all that?" Her response was life changing for me. She said, "I like you more because you were totally truthful. That made me know I can trust you to speak truth even if it is scary or hard." That was the moment I fell in love with Marci! For the first time in my life I felt safe with anyone...especially a woman! I had never felt that kind of love and acceptance! I knew that I wanted her in my life forever!

By the way...I said a quick prayer of thanks to God for prompting me to without guile from the start. Guile in Hebrew means mask. I learned to be with our mask and that trust is THE number one ingredient in a love relationship. I made a commitment to always be truthful...without guile no matter what.

Back then, Marci was, indeed, a beautiful woman...inside and out! She had all the attributes that every good man wants. Almost four decades later I am still madly in love with her.

And things have changed! Her face is still stunning to me but she does not look like a model and...I caused most of the changes in her body from what she looked like when she was 25. You see, we decided to have a family so I did my part by making her pregnant four times. Having a baby changes a woman's body. Weight gain is often one of them.

We men, and the world at large, including other women, should be less concerned about a woman's physical body and shape and more concerned about and interested in things that _really_ matter. Things such as her character, her spirituality, her attitude, her personality, her perspectives, creativeness, her brain power, her talents, her sense of humor, her ability to love and forgive, her ability and willingness to take care of her husband and family any way she can.

All of those things I just listed are within her and THEY are what matter. Not the shape of the body.

I love and enjoy Marci and want to be with her no matter what she is wearing, whether it be workout sweats or nice clothing and classy jewelry, with or without make up etc...When those kinds of priorities and right thinking are in a man's heart then you know that his love will stand the test of time and changes that occur in the body.

A man should love a woman for reasons that are at the highest level of the heart...not for shallow reasons like what her weight and shape is, her hip or bras size etc...

I experienced all of these with Marci those many years ago and continue to be blessed by her persona, her character and attitudes about life. And, yes, she is not the same shape as when I first saw her but THAT is okay for that is not the reason I fell in love with her and want her around me forever and ever.

I wish the word "hot" or "sexy" were never used to describe a woman. Other descriptive words are more important, accurate and complimentary and fit most of them regardless of bra size or body shape. Words like, kind, brilliant, trustworthy, sharp, funny, fun, sweet, interesting, cute, powerful, good, intelligent, loving, forgiving, creative and yes…beautiful. She doesn't need an hour glass figure to be beautiful.

Women have been blessed from above with wonderful attributes that are far more important than curves and physical attributes and abilities. They can be a tremendous source of joy and happiness and fun…a port in the storm…no matter what their size or shape!

I am so glad I fell in love with Marci from the neck up because from the neck down changed and I caused it.

Finding Sexiness No Matter What
By Janice Ogata

I had breasts when I was 10 years old and the figure of a woman. I was just a child when puberty hit. I was emotionally unequipped to handle all the unwanted attention from men. At eleven I was molested and at nineteen I was raped. I won't go into the details of my traumatic experiences, but what I can say is I thought if I didn't have "the body" then perhaps men would find me unattractive and leave me alone.

So that's when I began to overeat. I thought if I was chubbier, heavier, larger, then I would not be so appealing to men. However, I was wrong!

Beauty and sexiness come in all shapes and sizes. Even as I began to put on weight men still approached me. In the "real world", outside of Hollywood some men find plus-size women sexy.

It's taken me many, many years and countless therapy sessions to become comfortable with what I look like and to feel sexy in the body I have now. I believe sexiness is a state of mind. When I feel confident, powerful and happy I feel sexy. Sure we all have our insecurities, but deep down inside sexiness radiates from truly liking yourself. What you might think of as a flaw on your face or on your body a man may find very, very attractive.

What I've learned is beauty is subjective. One man may find me to be sexy, while another man might think I'm too fat for him to date. I prefer to call myself voluptuous, it sounds so much better.

Recently I was in a wonderful relationship with a man who was twelve years younger than me and he used to tell me how beautiful, gorgeous, and sexy he thought I was, every time we would go on a date or get together at his place for a lovely romantic evening.

I believe I was able to attract a much younger man because of my attitude. I *thought* I was sexy so I projected sexiness which he found irresistible. We dated for almost one year until our age difference became an issue for him. He left me for a woman closer to his own age, but I have never felt sexier than when I was with him.

Currently as a single woman I still do my best everyday to make myself feel good. I wear sexy lingerie (even if it's just for me), I put on perfume, apply makeup and dress in a style that I like. I enjoy big bold jewelry and bright colored clothing. I'm friendly and nice to others and I try to brighten other people's day by offering them a kind word or a smile.

Now that I'm older and wiser I would cherish "the body" I had as a 10 year old girl, but I realize I won't ever look like that again because I'm still an emotional eater and I am satisfied with the body I have grown into. It's been a long journey, but I have found my sexiness, no matter what!

Chapter 6

"In the name of the Father, the Son, and the Sexy lingerie"

"I never knew how to worship until I knew how to love."
—**Henry Ward Beecher**

"This is my simple religion. There is no need for temples; no need for complicated philosophy. Our own brain, our own heart is our temple; the philosophy is kindness."
—**Dalai Lama**

"Let your religion be less of a theory and more of a love affair."
—**G.K. Chesterton**

"Spiritual relationship is far more precious than physical. Physical relationship divorced from spiritual is body without soul."
—**Mahatma Gandhi**

"Science without religion is lame, religion without science is blind."
—**Albert Einstein**

I am curious in many things. My curiosity made me want to know more of whatever intrigues me. One of the things is the influence of religions on sexuality. We all know that religions are very spiritual while sexuality is very physical, so some ask if they are even related. On the contrary, some believe that sexual behavior is the tool to bridge the gap between the spiritual and physical. To me, I believe that the influence of one's religion has a huge impact on his/her sexual behavior–whether it is pushing them further apart; or pulling them closer together. Different religions such as Catholic, Mormon, Buddhism, Muslim... view sexuality in a very different way–they set their moral codes that discipline the mind, the behavior, the emotion....

I am curious to know why, in the old days, that the Mormons had one husband and many wives. I want to know why the Muslim women cover themselves from head to toe. I want to know why the Indian married women have the red dots between their eyebrows. These are social and cultural phenomena, but I believe they are very much influenced by the fundamental belief within their own religions. I have heard that the religious view sexual behavior, or any kind of sexual thought, as dirty and sinful. They practice sex with only one purpose in mind-reproduction. I have heard that there are religions that required individuals to separate their bodies from their minds and spirits when having sexual practice. If these are true, I guess the word "sexy" is far from their religions principle; or I doubt if it even exists in their dictionaries?

I was one of the mentors of the "Sisters" group which I gave guidance to teenage girls who are attending high school. We want to help or give guidance to whatever they face in life-friendship, school, communication, sex, etc. Knowing that these are sore subjects for most of them to share with their parents and hard to get a solid answer from their pals; the "Sisters" group develop a team of "big sisters" to lend them a listening ear, a light house to their journey and a short cut to their success. I heard from many young individuals, no matter which religions, have inherent shame, fears, misunderstandings and guilt about any kind of sexuality. Even the thought of "sexy" is a big secret. In fact, their beliefs of the term "sexuality" has been so narrowly defined that they forget that it actually includes not only sex; but also the diversity of sensuality-intimacy, identity, health, and reproduction.

It is time for a change! In the era of the Millennium, we should have a better understanding what we can do to improve our sexual relationship within one's religion. The era of *Religions VS Sexuality* should come to an end. Instead, whatever religion, it has to influence their followers that they should not feel shameful or burdened by their bodies. It has to educate them to appreciate and love their bodies because only through this, can one encourage a respectful attitude towards their sexual relationships. It can then connect your body and soul together.

I have also seen and heard about how people realize the power of sexuality; so they misuse it to manipulate, influence and control others. This is wrong and unfair to the human being and to the society. The harmful and destructive result can destroy one's spiritual and physical development. We should embrace intimacy as growing and healthy activities in enhancing one's self development.

It is not right to use sex as a trophy, or, on the contrary, as a threat or any kind of punishment in a relationship. All too often, we seem to accept a woman who uses sex as a reward. "No Sex" as a punishment to her man for whatever she is unhappy about. Sexual activities should be a channel to nourish love and pamper one's mind, but not a tool to manipulate one's desire or emotion.

If the main ingredients in Sexy DNA are "happiness", "Confidence", "sense of humor", "self love" and "mind set", so it means that no matter what your religion, as long as you have these elements, you process sexiness within. Stop treating "sexiness" as dirty, sinful and secret. Having a positive attitude towards what is sexy, not only will build the foundation of your spiritual development stronger, but also ultimately unite you body and your holy soul together. Because only when you allow yourself to appreciate the natural needs of your body and mind, then you can embrace the health, justice and mutuality.

Why don't men cover their faces?
By Hind Aleryani

We used to play in my aunt's garden when we were younger…girls and boys, there was no difference…we grew up together…we used to race, play, laugh…sometimes we would fight playfully…we used to watch TV together…cry at the end of sad cartoons together…we grew a bit older…we began to study for our classes together…whenever we'd fight we used to threaten the other that we'd tell on them to the teacher…we used to play practical jokes on one another…we'd laugh with all our hearts…

And so the days went by…

My cousin and I are staring outside the window…we are looking at the garden where my male cousin and his friends are playing…this is the garden where we used to play together…they used to be our friends once upon a time…these are the boys we used to play with… what happened? Why are we prisoners at home, while they play ball outside with all freedom…what did we do? Did we grow older? Did our bodies change? Did we become an object of temptation that needs to be covered from people's eyes? Aren't those the boys we knew since we were children? What changed? Why are we strangers? Why do I run and hide whenever I hear one of their voices? Is it just because the pitch of his voice changed? Is that why we aren't friends anymore? Are we supposed to act differently towards one another? Different to how we acted just yesterday? We started to act shy and anxious whenever we'd speak…we stopped playing with one another…My cousin and I began spending our spare time watching Mexican soap operas, as if we were in our 50s…

And so the days went by…

I am at school…we are learning about what a woman should cover… her hair is temptation…her eyebrows are temptation…I remembered my favorite male singer…his eyes were beautiful too…his hair is beautiful…why doesn't he veil? I asked myself this question, however, I couldn't find the answer…I remembered that I was banned from playing in the garden because I hit puberty…however, my male friends weren't…didn't they hit puberty too? Why weren't they imprisoned at home? I also couldn't find the answer…

And so the days went by…

I hear it all the time…"A woman is a jewel that needs to be protected (i.e. covered)"…and sometimes it is even said that a woman is like candy "if you remove the wrapper (i.e. the cover) the flies will swarm around her"…I turn on the TV and find that favorite male singer that I am so fond of brushing his soft silky hair and flaunting his handsomeness… his arms are bare…his chest is bare…why isn't this object of temptation covered? Why isn't he imprisoned at home? Why aren't women tempted by him? Some might claim that a woman shouldn't look at this…then shouldn't men shield their gaze when looking at a tempting female "object"? I couldn't find the answer…

And so the days went by…

I am at university…I see some people distributing a small religious book…"Temptations of a Woman"…Her hair…her feet…her eyes, and "thus, a woman must cover one of her eyes as both of them together are tempting"…I swear this is what I read in this book!…it's as if there is nothing left in this world to talk about and scrutinize other than a woman and how she is a temptation…I decided to observe men's looks…I wanted to know which women would attract men with her temptation… in front of me walks a woman wearing a tight Abaya (long black cover)…aha! I found her…she is an object of temptation…I continue watching…in front of me walks a woman with a baggy Abaya, however, with an uncovered face…the man stares at her…aha! So her face is also a temptation…a third woman walks in front of me…her face is covered and she is wearing a baggy Abaya from top to toe…the man is staring at her! Huh? I don't understand…what is so tempting about a black Abaya? No eyes, no feet...What is this man staring at? At that moment I realized that clothing has nothing to do with it...men would stare on all occasions...however, he, with his broad shoulders and his hair, eyes and lips isn't considered an object of temptation, even if all the women in the world started at him...*he is a man*...he shouldn't hide in his home... no one calls him a jewel...at that moment I wished I wasn't a jewel. I wished to be a free man....

And so the days went by...

I am in a Western country...women are walking around me...one is wearing pants...the other is wearing a short skirt...another wears shorts...men and women are walking side by side...it is strange...no one is staring...why don't I see the looks of men I saw in my country? Those looks that made a woman feel naked...those looks that I hated... the ones that made me hate being on this earth, and hate being born a woman...those looks that deny me my humanity...why don't I see those looks here? All the women are dressed up...why don't I see those looks even though all the women are attractive here? I saw one women run and laugh...I remembered that I wasn't allowed to run once I hit puberty...I remembered my aunt's window...I remembered I was an object of temptation that must be covered...I remembered that a man in my country wears white, while I am covered in black...I asked myself, why don't men wear black? Why don't men cover their faces? And I couldn't find the answer...

And so the days *go* by...

Levi's, Cowboy Boots and Tee Shirts
By Kathleen DePuydt

"Sexy" has had many boundaries for me. My childhood experiences and my interpretation of the many religious sermons and parental conversations I heard or overheard, all helped me develop a negative attitude towards my sexuality, self-worth and self-image.

In my early teens, when I wore my favorite clothes, boot cut Levi's, cowboy boots and tee shirts, I felt like I owned the world. I would walk into the house with my boot heels striking the floor sounding like a cowboy walking across a saloon's hard wood floor. To my mom, however, my footsteps sounded like my dad's, "Louie, is that you?"

"No, Mom, it's Kathleen."

It made me feel so grown-up to be mistaken for my dad. Those boots, jeans and tee shirts were my strength, my armor, and the only clothing I could actually fit in. I was as skinny as I was tall.

At a very early age, I recognized an inequality between boys and girls. When I was very young, possibly around the age of four, I viewed life this way:

1. You could stay indoors and do girlie things, or you could go outdoors and do real things. I chose the latter.
2. Secondly, there were boys, there were girls and then there was me. I knew I was a girl but I was not going to do girl things, play with dolls, have tea parties or dress up. No, I was going to do what boys did.

It was through my outdoor adventures that I met up with LJ. He and I were both five years old when we started the exploration of each other's bodies.

For the first few years, I found our new game tremendously fun; a clandestine adventure that was extremely pleasurable but when I was seven I had serious doubts about what we were doing. Around this time, I was well into my Catholic studies and knew the confessional was the place to take my secret but my imagination was more convincing than the perceived comfort I could possibly receive by confessing.

Upon hearing my sin, the priest would run out of his confessional booth, his vestments flying out behind him as he raced to my mom who would be kneeling in the pew. He would lean over and whisper into her ear and my mom's reaction would be complete horror. She would scream and start crying. The priest would come back, yank me out of the confessional, and the two of them would drag me out to the car. I would be banned from the church and my house for life for being such a bad, dirty girl.

I told LJ I didn't want to play anymore. He wasn't happy and said, "I'll tell the other kids."

"Go ahead, TELL!"

A couple of days later, LJ came up to me with his two best friends. They were pointing at me, poking each other with their elbows and laughing. "So what's it like kissing and 'doing it' with LJ?"

My heart, I swear, stopped beating. My stomach knotted up. I had to do something to get out of the situation. Since LJ was known to be a habitual liar and was not well liked, I decided to use those facts against him.

"Really, the two of you are you going to believe him? You both know that he lies all of the time. If you try to tell the other kids this made-up story, you know that they will laugh at you because nobody likes you guys. That's why you have to be friends."

Every day after that incident, I worried that someone would pull me aside and say, "You'll never know what we heard today?" Nothing was ever said again, but my fear never subsided.

Around the age of eleven, I started to experience periodic episodes where my undeveloped breasts ached and itched. This frightened me. After much thought and worry, I decided to approach my mom. I went into her bedroom. She was sitting on the far side of the bed reading, her back to me when I walked in.

"Mom?"

"Yes dear."

"Why do these itch so bad?"

"What itches, dear?"

"These."

She had to turn around to look at me and as soon as she saw what I was pointing at, her head snapped back to the book. She shook her head, stood up and marched out of the room. Since she never came back or bothered to answer my question later, I was devastated. It felt like she was validating the belief that my body was disgusting and sinful.

By the time I was 13, I had a 25-inch waist, a 35-inch inseam and an arm span that I thought only boxers would love to have. Buying clothes was a traumatic adventure because all dress slacks would fall below my knees like high water pants. Blouses and shirts with long sleeves would leave 2 inches above my wrist uncovered. Dresses would hang on me like an oversized pillowcase.

I felt so odd and out of place because I was taller than all the boys and male teachers at the school I attended. Even the few times I wanted to dress like a girl, I couldn't find the clothes to fit me unless my mom made them. Since sewing was something girls did, I never learned how to sew. Instead, I took refuge in my newly found jeans, cowboy boots and tee shirts.

My shame continued to grow especially when my mom started to leave little Catholic booklets on my bed. These informational pamphlets were written specifically to educate a young girl about her soon-to-be arriving monthly flow. All they did for me was land an additional blow to my self-worth. One section, in particular, was dedicated to the proper etiquette when hosting a dinner for that special young man you would date sooner or later. The instructions were quite clear that it was of utmost importance to place a white tablecloth on the table, least he think you were not a virgin. The booklet's content did nothing more than make me feel like I was permanently stained in menstrual-red sin. By this time in my very young life, I firmly believed that my virginity had already been lost because I had felt pleasure with LJ.

In my senior year in high school, the biology teacher had designed an 18-week science course that would focus on human anatomy and human sexuality, but students could only attend if their parents consented. Mine did not. I was crushed. The reason my mom gave me was that she didn't want me to learn about sex from a teacher who would not provide a Catholic perspective on the subject. Besides, I was to learn about this at home.

I screamed at my mom, "And just when are you going to start teaching me this? When? All you have done is given me pamphlets to read. Do you want me to learn about this in the gutter?"

This heated conversation took place in front of my two Catholic friends whose parents did consent. A day later, my mom relented.

Attending that class busted my childhood perceptions when I learned how birth control worked, what virginity meant, and the biological purpose of the menstrual cycle. Unfortunately, the class wasn't designed to deal with the psychological and emotional side of sexuality, nor was there any adult I trusted enough to tell them how awful and dirty I felt. As I started to mature, I felt more ashamed of my developing female body. I wanted to hide it especially after hearing comments made by female adults about the way certain other women looked, "That woman is just asking to be raped by the way she dresses," "She must be a tramp. Why else would she wear her skirt so short, and show cleavage?"

"Showing that much skin will end up unleashing some man's urges. It will be her fault."

It took me a number of years before I realized that the only relationships I truly enjoyed were the friendships I had with women. One in particular ended badly when I asked her if we could spend one weekend hiking together without her adult children and grandchild. This lead to a heated argument that ended with her telling me, "They are my children, and have you ever thought that they may want to see you as well as me. If you don't like them coming over every weekend, you can just move out! As a matter of fact, you need to move out."

I was crushed. It was very obvious that this relationship that had reached the far wall of platonic.

Two months later I moved to Northern California where I started living the life I was meant to live. At the age of 40, I accepted the fact that I was gay, and boundaries I had built around my own self-worth and self-confidence began to crumble.

The game-changing element was when I met my partner of 14 years. Seeing her walk into an Etta James concert and sit directly in front of me, I fell in love with her presence. She did fill out her jeans and tank top in an eye-pleasing manner, but that wasn't what drew my attention to her. It was her confident demeanor and staggering hazel green eyes that danced when she smiled. She was bold, energetic and sexy.

Appreciating sexy when I laid my eyes on her was easy but I admit, I still found it hard to appreciate my own sexiness. After I started dating this woman and accepted the fact that she genuinely loved me, and I loved her, things changed. The sensation I would get when her eyes would lightly touch my body, looking at me gently and slowly finally made me come of age. It made me feel like I was wearing my favorite childhood jeans, cowboy boots and tee shirt: strong, confident, and sexy.

'Sexy with No Boundaries'—
In the eyes of an American-Muslim Woman
By Sarah Khan

To me, the word "sexy" does not necessarily imply being provocatively dressed or having the type of unrealistic ideal body image promoted by the media. I am an American-Muslim Woman who covers herself from head to toe when in the company of all men other than my husband and close male relatives. This adherence to my faith's promotion of modesty and humility defines "sexy" for me as simply being "true to who YOU are, being yourself". It means being covered and confident, both in the attire I choose and the attitude I carry. Being a former fashion designer, I can assure you that it is surely possible to be modest and fashion-forward at the same time.

I recall the day my husband & I met for the first time, 11 years ago. I was dressed modestly, yet chic, in my hot fuchsia & cream polka dotted headscarf, a classy long neutral skirt & top, paired with a beige cardigan, and jewelry to pull it all together. That day he said "I have never seen anyone who can pull off Modesty so Fashionably!" We've been married for 11 years now, & every time we go out together, there hasn't been a day when he doesn't compliment me for looking sexy.

Thus, the term "sexy", in its true essence, indeed has NO boundaries!

Chapter 7
Your Royal Highness,
King Sexy!

"The *sexiest* thing in the entire world is being really smart, and being thoughtful, and being generous. Everything else is crap!"
—Ashton Kutcher

"Clothes and manners do not make the man;
but when he is made, they greatly improve his appearance."
—Arthur Ashe

"I think the sexiest thing on anybody is intelligence.
I respect somebody who has a brain and wants to
use it more than a pretty face and status."
—Sophia Bush

As previously stated, _"Old school sexy"_ never mentions the sexiness in males, which I think is not fair to the men. Why do we cherish and embrace male sexiness nowadays? I guess it is because women are more independent, out-spoken and open minded. We no longer just talk about men amongst our best friends, but we openly talk about men in public-to the mass media.

The "Old school sexy" might want men to be tall and handsome; however, _"Sexy in the New Millennium"_ for men is kind of blurry because it's difficult to define. Most probably, it is the "charm" that mixes physical attribute with the quality within. If you have the God-given handsome looking features, or an eye popping body, or a magnetic voice, you will certainly draw attention and increase your level of sexiness. But it is not all, because the physical attraction can only last for a certain period of time, after that, it is the "inner charm" that holds on to the attraction. I realized that having charm is a skill set and it can definitely be developed.

I can't think of a better way to learn _The Art of Charm_ than from those charming men such as Sean Connery, Roger Moore, Pierce Brosnan, George Clooney, David Beckham, Bradley Cooper, Hugh Grant, Jude Law, Ryan Gosling, Hugh Jackman, Brad Pitt, Leonardo DiCaprio, Tom Cruise…What is the secret to make a beautiful woman smile? What is the secret to become _"girls want to be with him and guys want to be like"_? It all comes down to 10 basic behaviors:

1. Good Sense of Style

Those that have a good sense of style and adopt a certain classy and stylish look will definitely impress the ladies. Women don't need you to be Pierce Brosnan or a David Beckham, but trying to keep yourselves updated on the trends will certainly add an extra credit to your impression.

I remember the Italian fashion power house Miuccia Prada said, "Fashion is an instant language". Indeed, before you can open your mouth to introduce yourself to that lady, the way you dress already spoke for you. The reason that women appreciate well dressed/stylish men is the same reason that men like to date well dressed/stylish women. It is a no brainer! Who can resist an attractive man like Sean Connery?

Results from a survey conducted by Kelton Research for The Men's Wearhouse Inc. concluded that most Americans believe that men, who dress well, or have a good sense of style, not only are more attractive physically, but are more successful at work too. They believe they could earn more money if they learned to dress better. I believe that it is true in an indirect way. For example, a well dressed salesman closes far more deals than his fellow sloppy salesman, so, he makes more money too!

2. Well Manners

They think a man who has a good sense of style is sexier than one with a lot of money. Of course it has to be followed by all the inner qualities such as personality, humor, intelligence and confidence. We tend to gravitate towards men who are well mannered, have a respectful attitude and confidence. Now I have the image of Richard Gere in "The American Gigolo" in my mind! A super well spoken, good sense of style and well-mannered man is really very attractive!

Some men think that if they are rich, this will increase their sexiness. The old saying "I'd rather be a rich man's darling than a poor man's slave" might hold true while the man is the family supporter. But with increasing financial power nowadays, many women can support themselves, so this saying might not be reflecting the modern woman. In fact, women nowadays do not necessarily focus on a man's bank account, but on how well he presents himself, both physically and in his manner.

The size of the bank account is not necessarily equal to the value of the inner qualities. If one is richer in so many other ways, he is by far richer than his bank account. What I mean is his consideration,

kindness, helpfulness, respectfulness, unselfishness, supportiveness...
and, if you happen to find a man who has these kinds of qualities, that
is the sexiest man ever!

That answers the question-"How does that average looking guy
get such a beautiful woman?" Well, maybe the woman sees beyond
his physical looks and bank account and really appreciates his inner
qualities. So men out there, don't worry about not having the looks
of Brad Pitt or Hugh Jackman, as long as you work on your inner
qualities, you can attract someone who really loves you from the inside
and out. Any relationship that starts from this foundation will pass the
test of time.

Some young boys have some issues around "What are good manners?"
Does it mean that he has to open the car door for his girlfriend? Does
it mean that he has to pay for every single meal when they eat out? Is it
a must that he has to walk on the side that is next to the street? There
is no guideline on this. It all depends on what your girlfriend likes.
Some are traditional and like to be taken care of. Some are liberal and
want equality between the sexes, so they will prefer going 50/50. Your
experience with your ex-girlfriend may not be the same as your current
girlfriend, so be open and clear so there won't be guessing and doubting
and embarrassment. When you both agree on how each other wants to
be treated, you can enjoy the relationship and that is the best of all!

3. Well-groomed
Remember women are feminine and like to be being taken care of. We
will not trust anyone who can't even take care of himself. While men are
attracted by women who wear nice makeup, neat hair style, sexy nail
polish and soft heavenly skin; women are attracted by well groomed men
as well. Make sure that you take good care of yourself, from the face,
to the skin, to the hand, to the facial hair, to the feet...well trimmed
body, good hygiene from body odor to their breathe. You want to show

women that you prepare well and spent your time in putting yourself together for her. That is the way to show her your respectfulness and who can resist that?

4. Smiles and eye contact

Don't belittle the power of a smile and the sparkle in your eyes; they are always important elements in closing a deal and developing trust in any kind of relationship. Men look for beautiful sexy lips in women, while women look for a warm smile from the men. Men look for beautiful eyes in women, while women look for the spark in the men's eyes when they are communicating with the women. If you are able to combine these two traits, even if you are not as handsome as George Clooney, you will be put at the top of the list. Having a genuine, inviting smile and sparkling eye contact will display self-confidence and charisma, your women will feel so special, and for sure you will be the winner of conveying charm.

5. Be a listener

John Gray, the author of "Men Are from Mars, Women Are from Venus" once said, *"When a man can listen to a woman's feelings without getting angry and frustrated, he gives her a wonderful gift."* Women like to express themselves, when they find that their men will lend the ears to listen and the shoulder to lean on, they feel safe and it will build the trust. The trust turns into the bond; the bond turns into love. Love is blind, when she falls in love with you; you are everything, her King, her Prince, her fireman, her sexy idol!

6. Be confident

I think one of the biggest worries for a man, is to lose his hair. He is afraid that it makes him appear to be less of a man. Good news is that these days, women definitely fall for bald guys! "Bald men are hot! If they can carry it off with the same confidence, minus the insecurity, I guess we'd have a winner!" grinned Raiza Khan, a hairdresser. All you need is a hint of confidence to let you deal with balding. So I will say "Happy Balding!"

It is fair that both sexes appreciate the charm from confidence. However, there is a fine line between confidence and arrogance, so please do not be fooled by that. Also, some men like to control or conquer and subdue their women. Some women misinterpret that as caring. I believe that it is the result of insecurity. So women, please don't let this type of man manipulate you! Confidence and charisma are the characteristics you should be admiring, not controlling and manipulating!

7. Sense of Humor

Most of the women appreciate men who have a sense of humor. Who doesn't want to be surrounded by the person who can make them smile or laugh? Funny guys are attractive, smart and often creative. They have the ability to *"think outside the box"*. One has to be smart enough to understand another's point of view, to have that "double vision"! All these traits make up a man's sexiness.

Humor not only can add laughter to a boring situation, but it also diffuses tension in an awkward situation, and thus reduces conflict. It helps in maintaining a longer relationship.

The best way to show your sense of humor is to be able to make humor out of what's going on in the moment. Some women even believe that a sense of humor is so important that it surpasses qualities such as intelligence, passion, confidence, and generosity. After all, everyone wants a partner who is entertaining and fun.

If you have the problem of giving dry, sarcastic humor; try using the most powerful kind of humor of all—make fun of yourself. Women love people who can laugh at themselves and their own mistakes. When you use a hint of self-deprecation, you are diffusing your ego and inviting her to get to know you on a deeper level. Women are born to nurturing, kind and sympathetic; so most of them are attracted to those men that are a little self-deprecating. The key is to show one's slightly self-effacing nature but ultimately kindhearted character, women will fall for that. Make sure that while you are saying something negative about yourself, make it clear that you don't really mean it. Women love humility and confidence! That is the greatest charm one can find, it is like a giant magnet! But make sure that you don't over-do, otherwise, your woman will think that you lack confidence. So one who uses this technique should really master the skill and know where the borderline is.

8. Protective Image
For those women who were raised by protective fathers or brothers; or who lacked masculine protection during her childhood; she would be attracted to someone who has presented this protective image to her. It can be seen as kind, rough, tough, or a combination, if the male demonstrates this "hero image"-he can easily attract women because some women, no matter how successful and independent they are, still have that sense of wanting to be protected deep inside of them.

In the back of some women's minds, they are equating those fatherhood figures as a good father for their children. Don't be shy to show that you care for your women, from little details as holding their hand while walking down the road, cautioning them about the uneven surface of the street; and making sure that they arrive home safely after they went out with you…it all show that you care for them and women love it!

9. Passionate
This one is interesting! Wonder how the Italians got their nick name as Latin Lovers? Why so many women are crazy for that? The passion! They are known to be passionate! Whether they are yelling crazy at the football

stadium; or screaming in front of the TV watching car racing *Formula Uno*; or going all out to show you how much he cares for you; these all come down to one word-passion! Women are attracted to passionate men. Women will not be attracted to boring men, when you have no interest in anything, women will pass you by very quickly. Whatever you do-from playing music to home cooking, to mountain climbing, showing her your excitable side will definitely arouse her interest in you.

10. Sincere

Growing up in a society that promotes "Heroes don't cry", it is hard to imagine how the concept of "Hero" is being changed. Instead of judging a crying man as being "weak", we are more interested in his sincerity. Nowadays, most of us believe that when men cry, it shows their vulnerability, a willingness to show their true feelings, being authentic. He is not afraid to show real emotion to his woman. Moreover, most women will be touched and it will melt her heart. It is one of the most powerful characteristics. Of course, one cannot always cry, otherwise, he becomes a mommy crying little boy that no one wants.

Men, if you practice these 10 traits, you will soon be named as "Mr. Charm" that exudes sexuality and beyond.

Recipe for Sexy
By Helen Woo

My recipe for *Sexy* is an equal mix of these ingredients…
- Self Expression
- Self Esteem
- Sense of Humor
- Love and Passion
- Integrity
- Kindness and Generosity

Self-Expression

"Action expresses priorities."
—Mahatma Gandhi

"It is obvious that I live life to the fullest because you can see it."
—Helen's "Wooism"

I express myself with:
- Words — I say what I feel. And I mean what I say.
- Clothing — I admire what I see. And I like it on me.
- My walk — I exude confidence, and it shows.
- My eyes — I give one look and reveal my passion.
- Touch — I welcome intimacy. I am affectionate.
- Laughter — I am happy. I feel forever young and healthy.

I am in touch with my senses and comfortable in my own skin. My expression is the MUSIC in my life.

Self-Esteem and Confidence

> "Belief actually creates the actual fact."
> —**William James**

> "I believe in myself. I have the power to create my own outcome."
> —**Helen's "Wooism"**

I AM

Funny	*Generous*	SMART
Persistent	**Sexy**	Loving
Resilient	Real	*Tender*
Strong	**SEXY**	Kind
	Passionate	

And I AM worth it!

Because I am worth it:

- I can accomplish anything.
- I can conquer the world and still stay true to myself.
- I have a message, and I plan to share it.

I gain confidence and increase my own self esteem when I collaborate with others who appreciate and use their own gifts and talents. I learn from their knowledge and wisdom. I gain confidence, so knowledge is *sexy*. It gives me strength to conquer whatever challenges may come my way. Strength is *sexy*.

Sense of Humor

"The human race has only one really
effective weapon, and that is laughter."
—**Mark Twain**

"A sense of humor is a powerful tool. Use it well,
and make me laugh. Sex appeal is what you have."
—**Helen's "Wooism"**

Laughter inspires me
Makes me feel good
Keeps me feeling young
Gives me hope, especially in times of distress
Makes me feel *SEXY*
Takes away pain
Brings joy to me and those around me
Is truly the best medicine for me
Gets me out of a "funk"
Takes me from a negative mood to a positive one in seconds
Brightens up my day
Plain and simple, laughing makes me happy
I have a quick wit and love to make others laugh too. What better way to go through life than with a smile on your face? I LOVE to laugh! People think I'm funny. I feel good about that because laughter is an important part of my life. And that adds to the *sexy* factor. It's impossible to laugh without a smile on your face, and a smile has such great sex appeal. So, *SMILE!*

I think the world is a better place with laughter. What does laughing do for me? I feel better about myself. I can look in the mirror, smile, laugh, and say, "I love me".

I can also laugh at myself. What good is it if you cannot? It makes for better relationships and adds an extra measure of *sexy* to the recipe.

I love a great sense of humor. I relate well to people who share the gift of a great sense of humor. Laughter changes my mood at any given moment when I have doubt. If I wake up stressed or worried about something, laughter lifts my spirit. And laughing makes me happy. You're never fully dressed without a smile.

Love and Passion

"Love is the master key that opens the gates of happiness."
—Oliver Wendall Holmes

"Get to know me, and you will be able to feel my heart AND look deep into my soul, for you will see nothing less than passion."
—Helen's "Wooism"

How do you love?

I love passionately, impulsively, with my words, with my actions and with my whole heart.

Love allows me to show great affection.

Love gives me great appreciation.

Love teaches me kindness.

Love makes me generous.

I give with love and with all my passion.

I love gently, powerfully, unconditionally, and completely.

Unconditional love is *super sexy*!

I am filled with love. And I am grateful.

Who do you love?

Love

*is patient
is kind
does not envy or boast
is not arrogant or rude
does not insist on its own way
is not irritable or resentful
does not rejoice at wrongdoing
rejoices in the truth
bears all things
believes all things
hopes all things
endures all things
Love never ends*

1 Corinthians 13:4.8

I love God. I also love the Higher Power within me. I nurture my soul by living by the "Golden Rule". All of the ingredients in this recipe feed my spirit. They help me bring the best of me into every moment of my life.

I love myself, my family and my friends. I love this world and the message I bring to it. My message to the world is to inspire others and to remind them that no matter how bad things get, there is a better tomorrow, and it's filled with love.

I love all my experiences and all my life lessons. I am grateful for them, for they have made me a better person. They have made me who I am. I love my life! I make every effort to live it as best I can. I enjoy doing things that I consider to be "special". I find that doing something special for myself keeps me happy and healthy. Caring for myself is a measure of love and is a necessity for me. When I take good care of myself, I can take care of my son, who means the world to me.

My son is everything to me and more than I ever imagined. I want to give him the best life I possibly can. With love and passion, I provide a comfortable home for him.

Taking care of myself gives me the ability to be of service to others. Service is an ingredient in the recipe, a part of love, kindness and generosity that creates my message which changes lives. *Now THAT'S sexy!*

Passion is a huge part of my life. I am passionate in all I do; when I work and when I play, immersing myself in everything I do. I am passionate about food. I enjoy savoring the flavor of every bite and experiencing the taste of every sip. Taste is very sensual to me. Food is a heavenly, exotic, indulgence. I am also passionate about staying healthy. My love of delicious food keeps me experimenting with healthy recipes so I can enjoy the flavors I love, while still keeping my body fit and strong. All of these things, big and small, keep me wanting and craving more.

I LOVE MY *SEXY* LIFE!

"There is so much love in your heart that you could heal the planet."
—Louise Hay

Integrity

"Be Impeccable with your word. Speak with integrity.
Say only what you mean. Avoid using the word to speak
against yourself or to gossip about others. Use the power
of your word in the direction of truth and love."

—Miguel Ruiz

"I find integrity to be the most important characteristic trait
in one's personality. Integrity is sexy. Therefore, I am sexy."

—Helen's "Wooism"

My word means everything to me. I say what I mean, I mean
what I say. And, I do not stray. I believe in the truth. I also believe
in my character.

I choose to tell the truth. I stay away from denial because it is the
lie that tempts us to stray from our integrity. Denial is just an excuse
we use when we do not want to admit something we did wrong. It
keeps us from taking 100% responsibility for our lives. As I live my
life with integrity, I admit my faults. I admit defeat, and I admit when
I am wrong.

Integrity also gives me the personal power and the humility
to apologize for my actions or my words that may have harmed
another. With that, I am hopeful that I would never repeat the same
mistake again.

People of integrity are always aware that their words and actions are
part of their moral fiber. I will not allow my integrity to be compromised.
Integrity is extremely *sexy* to me. It is honor and complete honesty
manifested in words and deeds alike.

"Real integrity is doing the right thing, knowing that
nobody's going to know whether you did it or not."
—**Oprah Winfrey**

Kindness and Generosity
"Here are the values that I stand for; honesty, equality, kindness,
compassion, treating people the way you want to be treated and
helping those in need. To me, those are the traditional values."
—**Ellen DeGeneres**

"I have a clear conscience, because I know that I am kind."
—**Helen's "Wooism"**

I can sleep at night with a clean conscience because I live by the
"Golden Rule: Do unto others as you would have them do unto you".

Being a good person starts with treating others like I want them
to treat me. It is my moral belief that kindness starts with love and
understanding. We learn to care, give and nurture others, by adding
value and kindness to their lives without prejudice. And I invite you to
do the same. I have a caring heart, so it makes no difference if you are
royalty, or if you are homeless and living in the streets. I will still treat
you with kindness and respect.

My rule of thumb is this; if I have nothing nice to say, I won't say
anything at all. It is never worth it to hurt someone's feelings. And, if a
good friend is asking for my advice, or my opinion, I will offer it with
care. I want to be good to myself and others always. I hope others live
by the "Golden Rule" too, but regardless of how they treat me, I will
always be kind.

I show my kindness and generosity by being:

Integrity.

Integrity is a concept of consistency of actions, values, methods, measures, & principles, expectations, & outcomes. It can be regarded as the opposite of hypocrisy.

- warm-hearted
- understanding
- considerate of feelings
- charitable and giving from the heart
- gentle and loving
- gracious
- humble

"Be Kind to One Another."

—Ellen DeGeneres

Words mean everything to me. Words are powerful. My words describe me. Words are *sexy* when they are honest and kind.

These are the ingredients that make up my recipe for *sexy*. I want *sexy* in me, *sexy* in my friends, and I especially want *sexy* in my significant other. I will settle for nothing less than *sexy*.

These are the ingredients in my recipe for *sexy*....

- Self Expression
- Self Esteem
- Sense of Humor

- Love and Passion
- Integrity
- Kindness and Generosity

All of these traits are extremely appealing to me, and MUST be in my life, the lives of my friends and the people with whom I do business. Notice that these ingredients don't have a physical component. These are a combination of values and virtues.

Now, when it comes to the man in my life, we have to add a little spice, a few physical attributes and some heat in order for this *sexy* recipe to be complete.

> "I think it's sexy when someone makes a statement that says, "This is who I am. This is what I think is sexy"."
> **—Carmen Electra**

> "Sexy is your frame of mind."
> **—Helen's "Wooism"**

What makes a man "Sexy"?

How does he grab my attention?

He says one word that will make me ready to hear all that may follow.

He flashes one smile, emanating from his heart that makes my knees buckle.

He gives me one quick look that says "wow" and grabs my attention.

The ingredients that make up a SEXY man in addition to the rest....

He walks with a swagger that exudes a certain commanding attitude and charisma as he enters a room.

He is confident, yet not arrogant, and he has an air of humility about him combined with a charming personality.

He is funny, and he makes people laugh with his quick wit.

He is loyal and he loves his family and friends.

He is a man of conviction, and quite intense.

He is smart and he is able to carry on a conversation with anyone.

He thrives in his business, as he thrives in his relationships.

He is ambitious and strong.

He is kind, generous and loving. He gives generously, and receives graciously.

When he fails, he gets back up, and he starts again, working until he prevails.

He is a man of his word. He shows great integrity, and he never strays.

He is gentle, yet so very passionate.

He is real, and he has sex appeal.

He is *sexy* from the inside out.

His Love is *Sexy* and I feel *Sexy* too!

"Love is a force more formidable than any other. It is invisible—it cannot be seen or measured, yet it is powerful enough to transform you in a moment, and offer you more joy than any material possession could."
—Barbara de Angelis

"The absolute most passionate gift of nature is love. Love is life. Life is Love."
—Helen's "Wooism"

He admires me for being myself. I can be completely authentic with him, as he likes me JUST the way I am.

He loves me as a person, and he appreciates me as a friend. He praises me for my hard work, in everything that I do.

He enjoys my sense of humor, as he finds me quite funny. He laughs when I am silly, yet he knows when to take me seriously. He welcomes my enthusiasm, and relishes in seeing me happy.

He encourages me, especially when I need it most. He goes out of his way to make me feel special. I treasure the feeling of being showered with love. It's wonderful!

He applauds my character and my integrity. He understands my views and goals, and he supports me unconditionally.

He loves me in the morning, and he loves in the evening. He likes me in my scrubs, and he likes me all dressed up. I feel pretty when I am all made up, and he makes me feel just as pretty when I am not. He genuinely adores me, for just being me.

He shows me love and respect; he treats me like a queen. He compliments me often, as he looks and smiles at me. He is very patient and sensitive to my needs.

He respects me for being a strong woman, and he understands my sensitive side. He cherishes me for all the qualities that I possess that make me the woman that I am.

He is ambitious and often busy; yet he always makes time for me. He brightens my days with his sweet little gestures, like a note or a phone call to say, "I love you".

He is truly kind to me, and his love nurtures my soul. Love exists, and love is *sexy*. The love I feel from him makes me feel *sexy*, too.

Now, let's put a little Chemistry in the recipe mix:

There is an unexplainable, magnetic force that draws me closer to him. Our connection is undeniable. The attraction takes hold of me, filling me with desire. The chemistry between us is like an irresistible force of temptation. My resistance is broken down to one fact…He is *sexy…Really Sexy!*

He stimulates my brain and my imagination.

He is *sexy*. He is ideal. He turns me on in every way. He fills me with passionate desire.

When he holds me close and kisses me, I feel as though I am melting into him.

I feel his passion, with his kiss. His touch I cannot resist.

He is *sexy*. He is hot!

Be Sexy!

"Sexy is in the mind of the beholder."
—Helen's "Wooism"

Sexy is all in your mind:

SEXY is a way of being. It doesn't matter how good looking or how wealthy one is. It's not about designer clothes, or how much skin is revealed. *Sexy* is a mindset. If the ingredients of the recipe are not in one's character, the recipe does not work.

When all the ingredients are mixed together, ideally in equal measure, the result is *sexy*. Missing an ingredient? There is always room for improvement. Practice makes perfect, so have fun mixing it up.

This is my official invitation to you….

If you have it, use it, *Sexy!*

If you've had it and lost it, bring your *sexy* back!

If you've never had it and want it, bring your *sexy* on!

Nothing Feels Sexier Than
Your Own Firm & Fit Body
By Brian Kelly

Have you ever noticed that you've just washed your car and take it out for a drive that it just seems to run better/smoother?

A similar thing can be said of us. Whenever you've just gotten that new haircut, or you've gone out and bought a new wardrobe, or you just had a makeover. Don't you just feel renewed, invigorated, even more, shall I say, sexy?

Well, over time, your hair grows back, your wardrobe begins to wear and fade, and that makeover, well, it's gone the next time you wash your face. In other words, the results (and the wonderful feelings that accompany those results) are very temporary.

What if there was a way to make that renewed/invigorated/sexy feeling more permanent?

Does such a thing actually exist? I've got good news…YES, it does! So what is it?

Are you ready for it? I mean, are you REALLY ready for it?

Okay, here it is…it's just one word:

Fitness!

If you are fit now (right now), then you are already experiencing the daily, PERMANENT feelings of being renewed, invigorated and sexy. Let's face it, getting fit takes time, effort (sweat), dedication, and all-out commitment.

Now, I'm not talking about the "I'll go into the gym this week when time permits" kind of commitment. I'm talking about the 6-7 days per week, 1 hour per workout kind of commitment. Yes, SERIOUS commitment. The question is "how bad do you want it"? So let me ask you, just how bad DO you want it?

If you're okay with covering up on the beach, or buying additional clothing accessories to cover up those "soft" or "bulging" spots, then there's really no need to read on.

However, if you have a burning desire to see that six pack again, or to fit into those size 5 or 3 jeans once again, then there IS hope. Simply get started on a *consistent* workout regimen...then stick to it. Getting started is the easy part, but sticking to it can at times seem daunting. Life can sometimes get in the way. But what if I were to tell you there is actually a REALLY simply way to staying on track? What if you could find a way to overcome all of the usual excuses that often keep you from getting up off of the couch? Would you like to know what it is?

Of all of the fitness tips I've given, seen & read about, there's one that always stands out way above the rest of the crowd. It is THE absolute most important fitness tip I can share with you.

Okay, here it is. One of the best, most proven methods there is for helping you to stay on track and not skip workouts is this:

Get a workout/accountability partner.

That's it. Simply, yes?

Get a buddy, a family member, a co-worker, anyone who shares your desire to achieve a higher level of fitness, and set up a workout schedule that you both can agree on. Then, stick to that schedule.

Okay, so you may be asking what makes this THE one fitness tip that stands out above all of the rest?

Well, I can't tell you how many times I myself have skipped workouts simply because I had no-one holding me accountable. Whenever I had a workout partner, he would push me to get back into the gym whenever I indicated I wasn't "up for it today". And, this works both ways. Whenever he was feeling a little less than inspired to hit the gym, I would grab him by the ear and drag him in with me.

Now let me tell you, on those days that I absolutely did NOT want to work out...after my workout partner dragged me into the gym and we completed the workout, I felt absolutely FANTASTIC and was SO grateful to him for pushing me to get into the gym.

So, the end results? It's simple. Fewer missed workouts equal faster results, period. And you know what "results" translates into? A firmer, more fit and sexier YOU. Not only will you LOOK fantastic, but you will FEEL fantastic as well. You will find you have more energy throughout the day. Your mind will be sharper. Your level of happiness will increase. ALL of these wonderful benefits will contribute to a healthier, sexier you!

Want to look sexier? Want to feel sexier? Then make fitness a priority in your life. Don't put it off...commit to finding a workout partner TODAY and embark on a new, happier, and sexier life.

Chapter 8

United Color of Sexiness

"I'm black, I don't feel burdened by it and I don't think it's a huge
responsibility. It's part of who I am. It does not define me."
—Oprah Winfrey

"You don't fight racism with racism, the
best way to fight racism is with solidarity."
—Bobby Seale

"I have no nationality—the best possible status for an intellectual."
—Emile M. Cioran

I was attending a seminar where there were over 400 people in the large ballroom. One could easily have felt over-whelmed by the over-crowded audience. I, instead, was drawn by a young woman who sat a few rows in front of me. The reason she stood out from the others is not because she is tall; on the contrary, she is very average in height. The reason she stood out beyond everyone else was because she was bald!

Yes, I have to admit that nowadays, we women do appreciate bald guys; they are known for being sexy (which is quite contrary to the old days). I know men who have hair, but shave their heads because it is kind of sexy and we do appreciate it. So, my eyes were stuck to her head, I then realized that she is black. When I read fashion magazines featuring models that are totally bald, nice body shapes, beautiful shiny skin and most of them are black. Yes, I have to admit that African-Americans have very nice bodies, gorgeous dark skin color and their features are very dominant. The more I look, the more I see the beauty in her. I noticed that she has a very beautiful shaped head. Aesthetically speaking, her head has a shape that is next to perfect.

I was so attracted to her physical beauty that I wanted to know who she is, what does she do? Why is she bald? I started to imagine her from the outside to the inside. You see, nowadays, it's not uncommon to see women bald because they have gone through chemo therapy during cancer treatments. The side effect is to lose hair. Now I am wondering if she is a cancer survivor. Or is she such a fore-front fashionista? If I have to set aside what really is the reason, I told myself, she is very sexy! A woman totally bald, if it is not for health issues, I will say that she is bald and BOLD! She must be very confident of her look.

I still remember when I was young, I used to watch The Miss World and Miss Universe contests—where beautiful young girls compete with each other to earn the title of Miss World and Miss Universe! That was a time when I could just sit in front of my TV and watch all the beauties from different corners of the world. From the exotic Tahitian, mysterious

Middle Eastern, confident American, sexy European, voluptuous African and ritual Asian, each one of them has its own charm and beauty.

Due to my cosmopolitan up-bringing, I am used to being surrounded by the melting-pot of different skin tones and features. From the African beauty with dominate features, thick lips, big wide eyes, curvy thick hair and curvy body shape; to the Asian's high cheek bones, almond eyes, band hair style, and slender body; to the Caucasian with the hour glass curvy body shapes, light skin tone with a blush of natural healthy pink at the cheek, some with the mysterious freckles, blonde hair, blue eyes and sexy long eyelashes…I do believe that sexy can be found in every shade and tone. From the darkest brown to the lightest pinkish-white hues, there are so many varieties. It is truly the United Colors of Sexiness!

I heard that Tina Turner once said, "I never had that thing about being black. If the whole world was like that, maybe there would be more harmony and love." It holds true to a certain extent, but this is about how interesting and creative each one of us is. With the varieties, it just makes us more unique. I call it truly a "Limited Edition".

Living from the inside out
By Dian Bias

Sexy is a mindset, therefore sexy is a perception, a feeling or an observation. One person's sexiness may be another person's vulgarity. There are no norms but there are definitely standards according to "society". However, it is up to you to agree or disagree with these standards. I tend to make up my own. You should too. My question to you is: what does "sexy" mean to you? Remember, your answer will always be the right answer for you. No one can take this away from you and no one can tell you you're wrong. If you accept this fact, you will find freedom in all your beliefs.

Today, sexy means feeling good about myself, whether that translates to looking good on a particular day or knowing who I am deep down inside or helping someone overcome a painful relationship experience. If it makes me feel good, I feel sexy. And when I feel sexy, I walk a little taller, smile a little more and of course want to keep feeling that way. So I rinse and repeat everything that stirs up the positive energy within me or around me. But I didn't always feel good or sexy about myself. More to come on that.

Sexy is also about being confident in who you are, what you believe in and not allowing others to dictate your life. How do I know? Well, I wasn't always filled with amazing self-confidence, or felt I deserved a happy life or even had great self-esteem. My younger life was consumed with difficulty, pain and emotional voids. However, my mature life now is consumed with love, awareness and hope for the future. To understand my transformation, you must first hear my story.

I was born in Kuwait to a Lebanese mother and an Indian father. Welcome identity crisis number part #1 and feeling different. Who was I? Where do I belong? Why don't I look like anyone else? Why doesn't everyone accept me? Is there something wrong with me? Overcoming these issues took years of self-reflection and some therapy to get through it. However, because the internal turmoil was deep seated as a child, I felt unwanted and therefore, not beautiful in any way for years.

The next junction came when I was 12 and my father suddenly passed away from a heart attack. The only man who understood me and wanted me to be whoever I wanted to be. He pushed academics on all his kids but he knew I was special. I was great in school and even better in sports. I was daddy's little girl but now I was alone. My mother and I had very different views about who I should be as a girl. I wanted to be that tomboy who played soccer with the boys in the cul de sac and she wanted me to learn how to cook and clean because that was tradition. Enter in identity crisis part #2 and part #3. I was fatherless and now rebellious. An internal self-esteem meltdown had begun. Why did I have to be "traditional"? Why did my father leave me? Did I do something wrong? Why did this happen to me? I hated God right about now.

Fast forward through the college years of drinking and making some questionable choices, I come out at the age of 25. Even now at this age, I had never felt very attractive before because I never saw myself that way. Suddenly, I'm excited now because I don't feel like a freak anymore. I knew who I was and that definitely helped me understand much of my past. Now I had direction. Well, the excitement didn't last long. Once my family found out about my sexuality, they disowned me and asked me to leave the house. Identity crisis part #4 presented itself. What do I do now? Who was I? Where do I go? Why was I like this? Can I be happy like this? Who will love me? Should I try to change who I am? Can my family be this wrong? Do I even know for sure that I'm gay?

As the years went by, I had to learn how to be my own best friend and stand up for what I believed. After some difficult relationships with women, I became a hard person to love. But one person finally got through to me. She saw me for who I was and not just for my outward appearance. She taught me to see myself completely: mentally, emotionally and physically. It was a hard fought battle but I finally started to feel "sexy". I was now in my 30's and knew there was no going back to the way I used to think about myself. I loved who I was becoming on the inside. My confidence became stronger. My self-esteem did a complete 180. Understanding "who" I was according to "Dina's beliefs and standards" was all I ever really needed. Once I gave myself permission to be myself fully and completely without reservations, I knew "sexy" would always be a part of who I was. And it still is.

Today, I am on top of the world! I even became a Certified Life Coach and Mentor to help women understand who they really are on the "inside" so that they can live their lives with love, openness, passion and mostly, peace of mind. No one can keep you from being you, except yourself. Isn't it time you gave yourself permission to live FULLY?

How do you feel sexy?
By Svetlana Ray

Hidi, thank you so much for asking me this question! It made me think of more things than I could imagine.

First, I thought of the word "sexy". What does it mean? Does being sexy mean also beautiful? Does it have to be connected to sex? Is what sexy for one, also sexy for others? What is "sexy" today, will it also be "sexy" tomorrow? .And second, that question "How do I feel sexy?" surprisingly made me rummage through old memories. I thought of my childhood, the street where I grew up and my parents and grandparents. I thought of Bulgaria. You may ask: "What does "sexy" have to do with all this?"

Back there (in Bulgaria) and then (about 45 years ago) anything to do with sex was a taboo and "sexy" was a bad word. One could expect only punishment if they would bring up sex even as a secondary subject in a conversation.

However, I grew up thinking there was no danger for me in that manner. I was NOT beautiful; therefore I wasn't sexy either. I believed what my mom used to say to me when I was a little girl: "Svetlana, you are so unnoticeable…!" (Gee, thanks, mom!) Then she would add: "… But you have great charm when you talk!" (Parents, beware! This is how you plant mental filters and beliefs into your children's minds!). So, I never thought I could be beautiful or sexy! Thankfully, at least, I could be charming.

In high school I was a quiet girl, focused on my studies. Of course, I didn't expect to have a partner for the Graduation Bal (Party). A week before the event the greatest looking boy of the whole school, the dream of every girl, asked me if he could be my partner at the party. I was shocked. I didn't know what to think. I was afraid he was joking with me. But he wasn't. The evening of the party he would call me a "goddess" and he also treated me as such! He was such a gentleman! I was attended to any of my desires and I must say: his attention was so flattering. We were named "The Best Looking Couple" of the evening. All this was a BIG UNKNOWN to me. That night my face lit up, my behavior changed, I walked taller and I smiled more. The beliefs planted in my head by my mom's words were shaken.

Years later, after I graduated from Technical University with a Master of Science degree, and two extra majors–Journalism and Management and Marketing, I arrived to Los Angeles ready to conquer the world. But instead of stepping on a red carpet I landed on my butt and faced a miserably difficult beginning of my life as a new immigrant. I worked at whatever jobs were available to me. I was ready even to wash dishes. Nothing sexy about that! One day, trying my table-waiting potential in a Middle-Eastern night club, I heard music I had never heard before. A dancer came up on the stage and…a new magical world opened its doors to me. I fell in love with the music and I merely let it lead my body in a mysterious dance. I discovered a talent I didn't know I had–Arabic belly dancing! Soon I was offered a job as a belly dancer in that same place. It was a great proposition, simply because it was the only job offer I had at that time! Now, that was a challenge! Remember my mental filters and beliefs? Remember–"being "sexy" lead to punishment"? Oh, and I had to dance almost half naked! I hoped my family would never find out! I accepted! After all, my LOVE for the dance won over my inhibitions.

I remember when I went to buy my first costume. It was a cheap Halloween Belly Dancer's costume. I went into the fitting room to try it. When I looked in the mirror, I could not believe how beautiful I looked! It was as though if I had come out of my own dreams. But it wasn't me– it was the princess I always wanted to be! For a moment I thought there was something wrong with the mirror! I couldn't be so beautiful! But it wasn't the mirror. It was HOW I FELT! How I WANTED TO FEEL. It all came from the inside! I imagined myself on the stage, graciously moving, dancing in the rhythm, smiling to the people around me and radiating my own enjoyment. And it came true–I danced on a stage for more than 6 years.

I knew, in the beginning I didn't dance too well, but I didn't care. I FELT MAGNIFICENT!!! I simply ALLOWED myself to FEEL (not to look) sexy, beautiful, desired, attractive, charming, inviting, lovely, seductive, engaging, passionate, and much more! I was full of JOY! And that was what attracted the audience to me. Men and women would tell me what a beautiful and sexy dancer I was. But I knew–it wasn't the looks! It was the JOY that attracted them–the joy that was streaming out of my moves, my attitude and my smile.

To me belly dance was the art that revived the magic of my inner beauty. Speaking the love-language of the soul, it changed my life. It gave me a special kind of confidence and a new belief–I believed that the power to FEEL beautiful and sexy is within me. Indeed, it all begins within–with our decision, thoughts, imagination, love and passion. Looks? Of course we do the best we can with whatever Mother Nature has gifted us! The rest is our CHOICE!

Perhaps, my mom gave me a gift by telling me that I was unnoticeable. Thus, I really worked on bringing out what was already inside of me– love, joy, passion, and more love!

Now, as a therapist and a trainer, I do help people to remember that they have the power to bring that inner beauty out and let the world reflect their own magnificence back to them!

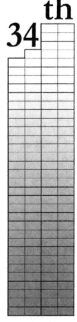

Sexy on the 34th floor

"Some women choose to follow men, and some women
choose to follow their dreams. If you're wondering
which way to go, remember that your career will never
wake up and tell you that it doesn't love you anymore."
—Lady Gaga

"Goddess is one part INNER Beauty, one part
outer beauty and one part 5-inch-high heels"
—Jennifer Lopez

I had a fond of leather since I was very young. My father was a tailor who specialized in leather jackets. I remember in our tiny house, we had a pull out table as big as our bed. It was his table where he would draw the pattern and cut the leather. The smell of leather filled every corner of the house and I was addicted to the fresh strong smell of skin. I felt a sense of femininity and yet very strong and powerful!

I remembered vividly my father used to ask me to stand still in front of him so that he can take a precise measurement of me. That must have happened a few times during the course of my up-bringing from junior to teenager. I wore leather jacket since I was very young, but not knowing that it was a luxury piece of outfit. Every now and then, I felt good being dressed nicely when my friends admired my one of a kind custom made leather jacket.

When it came to the final year of my fashion design course, the emotional attachment of leather inspired me to have my final collection dedicated to the appreciation of "skin". It was a women's collection made in super soft suede in pastel colors, inspired by the relaxed yet sophisticated life-style in Monte Carlo. Every now and then, I still recall the sophisticated models walking down the runway with the long pipes in their hands and backed with Bob Mackey's famous pop song from the 80's–"Don't worry! Be Happy!" That was my very first runway show!

Different fabric has different characteristics. Leather reminds me of the power of authority. The thickness of a calf skin shows me the character of tough, strong and persistence. However, the soft lamb skin speaks chic and elegant. Suede has a relaxed and down to earth feminine touch to it.

Because of my up-bringing, I fell in love with leather. Every time when I wear leather clothes, I feel the power and a dominant status. When I have any type of important meeting or presentation, I love to wear my leather outfit, the rich nature of leather makes me feel professional, confident and in the state of authority. However, to balance the masculine energy, I love to wear something totally different underneath. I love to keep myself feminine on the inside. A sexy boudoir set of silk lingerie spells femininity from head to toe. Pair it with a very traditional French cut garter belt with an intricate design stocking...I am in my own heaven! With that, I feel like Lynda Carter, the Wonder Woman-a super powerful sexy woman, with both masculine energy and feminine gracious. I think that is exactly what a modern woman should feel, especially when they are in the work force competing with the other men.

I believe in the balance of things-Ying and Yang, positive and negative space. Too much toward either side will destroy the harmony of the universe.

To be sexy and at the same time professional is a challenge to many career women. At one point, we want to show men that we are as capable as them, so we avoid dressing as a "weak" lead. So the answer is a socially accepted image as a professional woman-career suit, long pant suit or knee-length skirt suit.

But floating in a pool of "expected image" is kind of boring and it is hard to stand out from the crowd. That is what I say "Small fish in a big pond". Not to mention that most women are searching for their identities within the "expected image"-personal style. Some feel that with the career look, they are lack of femininity which they cherish. But when they dress to be more feminine, they face the jealousy from their female colleagues; or some face the disrespect behavior from the male colleagues.

So the question raised-Can we be both sexy and professional in our working environment? It is easier to a man than to a woman. For example, how many of you fall for the macho/heroic look from a policeman or a fireman? What about an image of a Navy Officer such as the one played by Richard Gere in "An Officer And A Gentleman"; or a sophisticated and professional pilot played by Leonardo DiCaprio in

"Catch me if you can"…those uniforms already speaks for authorities, power and professionals. The best of all, they are very attractive and sexy. These particular jobs offer both professional and sexy image, but for a woman, it is very hard to pull it off.

To say that it is challenging for a woman to be both professional and sexy doesn't mean that it is impossible. But there is a fine line between the "respectfully sexy" and the "disrespectfully sexy". For any creative career like mine, it is more acceptable to show up at work in nontraditional attire–believe me, I have way too many colleagues with tattoos, nipple rings, belly rings, crazy hair color…but many other professionals such as professors, physicians, lawyers, sales people…they do need to have a more conservative professional image. It is their image that helps them to build the "trust" within their professional work. I can see that they are more challenged in distinguishing themselves than the other careers. There are the invisible boundaries that they cannot cross. My advice to those professions for being sexy and professional at the same time, it will have to be a very subtle sexiness. It is a package that includes both internal and external.

Internal:

Remember when I talked about how important it is that confidence, happiness, a sense of humor, positive attitude and self-love are some of the major elements to magnify ones' sexiness? Positive attitude creates positive energy within the work environment. Love who you are, love what you do, love your boss, love your colleagues and love your pay check-no matter how big or small it is. In other words-count your blessing.

You are going to smile more, laugh more, joke more, you communicate in a positive manner to your colleagues and that draws the same people to you. This is the Law of Attraction. The harmony at work will create an environment of unity. When people like you, work will be more efficient. That is the air of sexiness; it is a feeling, not a visual thing. Feeling is powerful and don't belittle it.

No one can judge your sexy lingerie under professional attire. The best kept secret is the feeling between you and your lingerie. Knowing that you are wearing something sexy underneath will radiate the same message and it will change your attitude and mood. Try some luxury material like silk or modal or microfiber; try some vibrant color that make you feel fresh and cheerful; try some prints instead of solid colors; try some specially designed lingerie that make you feel over the top; try wearing a variety of lingerie such as a garter belt, waist cincher, bustier…to empower your femininity. Even though it is unseen by others, the power is in the mind. All of a sudden, your chin is up, head is up, chest is raised, you walk with confidence, you fill with energy, you are more alert, your mind is more creative you communicate more intelligently. What you feel about yourself is the most important source of sexiness. When you feel sexy, your vibe will align with you and that is the sexiest of all.

External:
The guideline of "respectfully sexy" and "disrespectfully sexy" is sometimes very blurry. It is like walking on thin ice. But if you understand how certain things are perfect only in a certain time and place, then you will know how to adjust your look in the work environment. You don't have to show "skin" in order to be seen as or feel sexy. You can achieve sexy or sensual or feminine in a professional way. Inappropriate wardrobe choices such as an outfit that is too revealing for a work environment will lead to unnecessary distraction, or even worse, send out wrong messages to the opposite sex, and thus lead to disrespect and trauma. Some experienced the risk of causing people to take them less seriously, and thus missed the opportunities of promotion or any further opportunity of their career development.

Trying to be both sexy and professional seems to be easier said than done. But as long as we are clear what is the guideline. We should have a pretty clear picture. Here are some tips to share my insight of how to project femininity while maintaining a respectful professional look. I call it "The Ten Commandments at Work".

1. No matter how you dress, *don't let the way you dress over-power your ability to perform your job.* The way you dress should be supporting you as a professional individual; instead of diverting your intelligence and integrity. If you follow this #1 rule, you will not only win the respect of your boss, but also eliminate the chance of jealousy from your co-workers.

I remember my brother told me the reason he fired his secretary. One day when he passed by her desk, he saw her holding two pens, one in each hand to type the keyboard-to avoid messing up her nail polish and mistyping because her fingernails were too long! She might have thought that she wanted to display her sexiness by showing off her hot and sexy long fingernails, but she had forgotten the my brother hired her is to work. She had let her image overpower her quality of work.

A few years ago, my boss hired a very curvy Hispanic secretary. She had very big tits and she dressed very provocatively too. I overheard that once she wore a super low cut mini-dress on a day when our major client came for a meeting. Literally, everyone's eyes (both men and women) were trying to find a place to land, instead of being distracted by her almost totally exposed breasts. They all had a hard time focusing on the meeting. There were mixed feeling of embarrassment, distraction and disrespect.

Next day, we got an office memo to "everyone" about the "dress code". It was the first and only time that the dress code was implemented. The hard part of this is that we are a fashion forward company. Dressing edgy and fashionable is part of the business. But it looked like the "respectfully edgy and fashionable look" was damaged by the "disrespectful look". Understand that the showing of a lot of cleavage or wearing the mini skirt so short that you almost show your crotch is an invitation to sexual thoughts-and not just for perverts. It's a distraction. At work, we want to focus on business so we can set ourselves to be successful. Any kind of distraction is the blockage of business growth.

2. I remember I read somewhere "People are hired because of their experience and talent, but are fired because of their attitudes". It is very true! Attitude is not everything, but it is very important. Employer will not know ones attitude when they looks for the right candidate, they can look for their education, experience...but until that employee joins the work force, then the attitude will show, and it can build or kill their career.

To practice having a great attitude means to speak, think and perform in a positive way. Everything you do is directed towards improving the business. It also means that we focus so much on improving ourselves that we do not allow ourselves to speak poorly of the others. We thrive on searching for innovative ideas to improve the quality of our products and to better service to our clients.

Having a great attitude also means that you are able to admit your faults. Understand that no one is perfect and so why should you be? We all learn from our mistakes and treat it as lessons to master our success. So often we find that when mistakes happen, people are just trying to put the blame on others. This behavior will not solve/improve the situation, and it will lead to anger within the environment. We should be so professional that we are able to be responsible to our work.

3. Simply let your high heel shoes work the magic for you! One day, my friend Helen stamped into my office with a glint in her eyes. She yelled out, "I cannot believe how high heel shoes make me feel so powerful and confident! It literally lifted me up! When I wear flat shoes, I feel small, sloppy and insignificant; but high heel shoes really can pull the trick!" I immediately thought of Jennifer Lopez. She once said, "Goddess is one part INNER Beauty, one part outer beauty and one part 5-inch-high heels" Yes, high heel shoes are magical! I remember seeing a 5'10" colleague wearing a 5" high heel shoes, and she looks like a giant to me! You would have thought that she doesn't need to wear high heel shoes; but it is not just the appearance; it has a very profound psychological impact to the wearer. Once you put on the high heel shoes on, all of a sudden, you exude femininity, power and confidence. Your body gesture is better; you walk like you are in the runway; you know that you are more attractive; you know that you are being noticed; you feel that you are more flourishing!

Thank you to Catherine de Medici (wife of the Duke of Orleans) who set the benchmark for the high heel shoes in the fashion empire in 1533! As early as in the beginning of the appearance of high heel shoes, it already set an exclusive to the higher class, I still remember even in the early 1700s, King Louis XIV from France decreed that only nobility can wear red colored high heel and that no one can wear heels higher than his. Since ancient, high heels shoes already was a sign of power, status and privilege; nowadays it rises towards sexuality and sophistication. As simple as wearing a pair of high heel shoes, you can add a lot of professional image and yet sexiness in the office. That is the easiest make-over!

One more important attire tip-the best way to enhance your body curve is to wear *well fitted clothes*, it holds true for both men and women. You will look more professional and intelligent which will directly encourage your colleague, boss and clients to respect your opinion. I also noticed that overweight individual tend to wear over-sized outfits. They think that when they cover themselves with a big piece of fabric, then their over-sized body will be hidden; instead, they only look even bigger and shorter! No matter what size you are, wearing well fitted (not tight fitted) outfits will show the best of your body.

4. No matter what features, color, size and age you are, *never down play yourself*. Stop complaining about how your body doesn't match up to your expectation or how you are not smart enough. Even if you are physically handicapped, trust that you are no worse than those that are physically healthy. The most powerful tool in a person is not their physical ability; it is what is in their mind. The reason that you are hired is because your company believes that you are capable of the position, so there is no need to belittle yourself. Be comfortable with your own skin, it is a major element of acquiring confidence. We need confidence to perform our best.

5. *Pay attention to the words that you use*. Swear word doesn't make you sounds more edgy, funny or powerful; instead, they only make you sound uneducated, unprofessional and disrespectful. Constantly putting others down does not really spell fun to the others. Some people like to use swear words or frequently weave sexual topic into the business conversation. They think that they are forward thinkers; they think that by teasing or verbally abusing their colleagues, they will be perceived as leaders or victors. Little do they know that it only shows how insecure they are. Instead of focusing their energy to their best

potential; they are spending all the energy and emotion to put others down.

6. *Avoid topics that lead to sexual encounters.* It is not a subject to bring to a professional business. Some think that weaving sexual elements into business will cause them to be perceived as funny and have a sense of humor. They think that making fun of others shows them to be superior, instead, it only shows how ignorant they are.

Never flirt with anyone in the office. Your colleagues, boss and clients are there to do business with, not to develop any kind of personal relationship. Having said that, I don't mean that you cannot go out on a date with your colleagues. It should not be shameful if you fall in love with your colleagues as long as you are not distracting the business environment.

7. *Too much make-up is really not suitable at work place.* When I face someone who is wearing way too much make-up, it just overpowers her speech. I focus so much on her make-up that her words just pass by my ear. It creates too much distraction at work. I still think that natural looking kind of make-up is the best. As long as you refine your skin tone with the proper foundation; put some blush at the cheek to make you look more refreshing and energetic, you will look natural and cheerful. Put appropriate eye makeup to make you look bright and lively; avoid the evening night club kind of make-up. You want to show that you come to do work, not just getting ready for after work entertainment. It makes others think that you are getting ready to party, instead of giving your full attention to your work. Make sure that however you present yourself, it doesn't distract from the quality of the work that you are doing.

8. Creative hair color/style, tattoo and body jewels are really very personal. I do have to admit that for an individual who works in the creative environment, it is more acceptable to have more vibrant hair color and tattoos. I have worked with many colleagues who have tattoos or body piercings. But I have heard that even in a non-creative work environment, there is a rising scale of this kind of personal identity. In my opinion, as long as you make sure that your boss/company do not take you less seriously just because of your "personal identity"; and that you have a great attitude, speak respectfully and are devoted to your work, then, I believe that you are no different from any others.

9. We all know that the #1 reason that leads to cancer is stress. Many people suffer from work stress. To avoid the high level of stress, one should practice great self discipline-that means understanding that focus, hard work and prioritizing is the core of being successful; it can mean that we should have complete control of our eating behavior; it can mean knowing how to balance work and personal life; it can mean that you keep yourself healthy so you can perform your best at work; it can mean that we should be able to bring it to your boss' attention when you are over-loaded and need extra help. We are professional and we should be able to handle the stress in a professional way.

10. *Dress your part!* I used to work with a fitting model for many years. She was beautiful, tall and had all the curves in the right places. She was our 34DD fitting model, just the perfect figure that we need for fitting purpose. She came at least twice a week for fitting. Every time when she came, she dressed very casual, wearing a sweat suit. She didn't pay much attention to her hair, her make-up or her shoes. I can easily understand her

reasoning. She knew that once she went into the fitting room, she was going to strip naked. But she didn't understand one very important fact-even though we paid her the professional rate, she didn't impress us that way.

In the meantime, she always complemented how I dressed. She was shocked that I dressed so meticulously every time she saw me. Then one day, she asked me, "Hidi, isn't it a lot of work to dress up like that every day?" I replied to her with confidence, "I am a fashion designer, so I have to dress like a fashion designer." She was a little still and embarrassed, "You mean that I am a model and so I have to dress like a model?" I agreed with authority.

Little did I know that a light hearted conversation between me and her became the motto of her future career! I met her a few years later at a seminar during which we learned how to write books. I was so surprised to see her there! "Why are you here?" both of us ask each other the same question! Of course, the answers are the same! We were planning to write a book! But this is not what I want to tell you. I want to tell you that she had completely changed from head to toe! She always had good posture, that's for sure! But her hair, her make-up, her outfit, her shoe… that is another person! She has totally up-graded herself and now dressed her part! She was just head to toe professional model material. I saw the confidence she showed when she spoke, the eye contact that she had when she was talking to me…I was very happy for her.

Few summer later, I learned from Facebook that she had her book out "Ultimate Guide to Style—from Drab to Fab". In this book, she taught how to dress. Not only that, she told me that inside her book, she told a story about me?!?! I scratched my head, not knowing what story did she recalled about me-until I met her again in another event where both of us were invited to speak as a panelist over the topic about fashion image.

She was so nice; she handed her book to me, and turned to the page where she talked about how I changed her life! The story was exactly the one that I mentioned above before about the conversation that we had inside the fitting room. She told me how much my belief had affected her professional development.

She finally realized that dressing her part gave her, not only the confidence, but also the trust from her clients. On top of that, she realized that she felt like she owns the world when she dresses nice.

Soon, she made sure that she dressed professionally everywhere she goes, even though she knew that once she walked into the fitting room, she would have to strip naked. She told me how her career just took off! The big corporation that hired her for fitting liked how she presented herself and they have lots of confidence in her. They started to give her clothes, and asked her to wear them like a mobile billboard! She started to have free fashion wardrobe supplies! Not bad at all, right?

Now, she really knows the power of dressing your part. In fact, the way she packages herself as a whole gives so much confidence to her clients that now she became an image stylist. She helps individuals to find their own style and dress for success!

Women should be able to be perceived as smart, intelligent, sexy and legitimate no matter where and when. I haven't forgotten those women who have a home based office/company. With the merging number of women entrepreneurs, there are many stay at home moms/house wives setting up their business in home offices. They communicate through the computer or telephone while doing their business at home. Since they think that they are not to be seen by anyone, they do not have to take care of themselves. They do not groom themselves, wear sweat suits, or even worse, rollers or curlers on their heads; oversized t-shirts with roomy big pants cover their bodies…they believe that they have no reason to dress up since they are not to be seen. They do not feel attractive or sexy—and they believe that they actually don't need that kind of lift-me-up emotion.

All these "not being serious" attitudes create an air of sloppiness. The image of "professionalism" is not on their minds. But if they dress as if they are going to meet the CEO; to present their products in front of a team of buyers-all of a sudden, they have better postures, better tone of voice, minds are more alert! Speeches become more powerful, thoughts become more creative.

I hope you keep these Ten Commandments near your work area and always remind yourself that YOU can be both SEXY and PROFESSIONAL as long as you practice these guidelines. All these attributes combined allow the growth in your business and career development.

Professional and Sexy
by Design within your Mind
By Jennifer Bagley

Sexy... from the inside out. Being sexy begins with a mindset. Being whole. Loving yourself. Your personal self image. When I look back on my professional career as a speaker, executive and entrepreneur, I think about how being sexy played a role in my success. With confidence I can tell you, much of my success has came from my own personal definition of being a professional sexy smart woman, strong from the inside out.

Hidi Lee asked me how important I thought being sexy was to my professional career and without hesitation, I said it is part of a foundation that everything can cling to. I believe that you attract what you are, not what you want, therefore, if you want to attract something different, you will need to change who you are from your core-which again, is simply the way you think.

Learning is the key to grow self image and your self-image is the foundation for your overall sex appeal. Learners will inherit the earth and run the world, while those who cannot learn, unlearn and relearn will die. What you learned today, may not apply tomorrow therefore if you hang on to what you learned today, you may be outdated and obsolete tomorrow.

Getting to where you want to be is NOT supposed to be easy, comfortable and safe! Nor is it going to be fast. But you must be consistent in your desire and commitment to become comfortable with being uncomfortable and with personal change.

Being truly sexy requires you to get out of your comfort zone and stay there as there are different levels of progress. I believe there are 4 levels of success in building the ultimate lifestyle.

1. Phase one is your own personal self image and sex appeal.
2. Phase 2 is you and your significant other's image and sex appeal as life partners.
3. Phase 3 is your family image and appeal.
4. Phase 4 is your network.

If your income and happiness is closely related to the 10 most integrated people in your life, then why not seek the total package?

Where to start…? I believe that, in order to free up the space to work on you, you need to start with the process of elimination. In my life, I focused on reviewing how I spent my time, what I spent my time on and who I spent my time with. And decided, less is more. Some would say that I choose not to have friends. Or I choose not to be entertained by TV and similar activities; however, I believe that I choose to realign my time closer to my goals, so I may experience faster growth.

First I had to gain clarity around what I want in life. Notice I did not say business. Remember, I choose to seek the total package…a network of people who think like I do and have similar goals. Am I there yet? No…I am still focused on phase 1, 2 and 3.

The way we habitually think under any given situation will provide a specific result. People are the result of their though habits. What they do is largely based on habits not out of conscious thought-I am focused on changing small things consistently which will cause things around me to become fundamentally different.

Did you ever notice that you hire people based on skills, yet fire people based on attitude? This is another reason to think about how important it is to have that sexy professional attitude.

For some, this may require a paradigm shift as your current frame of reference is based on your current and past experiences, influences and thoughts. The way you see the world is not the way I see the world, but rather the way you are. Change who you are and you will fundamentally change the world around you. The world does not change, however your paradigm shift will change the way you look at the world.

The great part is…it's a choice. Everything is.

Your attitude makes up your paradigm.

Get out of the comfort zone. Do the things you fear the most-this is how you grow. People fear being wrong-so people don't make choices, they allow life to rule them. Some people have the fear of needing someone else, so they never have the luxury of truly being in love. We have been conditioned to avoid fear and change. Therefore they step into change only to revert back to what's comfortable, taking 3 steps forward and 5 steps back.

I choose to create my own comfort zone-through continued growth-getting comfortable being uncomfortable is what I choose. This continuous growth is necessary in life-this must be your habit-to grow and change. It's difficult seeing people who I know have a desire to change, simply slide back into what's comfortable to avoid change, and many quit one yard before the touchdown, in love, life and business.

I have had many interesting conversations about being born sexy or being trained sexy. I strongly believe that, as is everything else in life, it is by choice. We are ultimately who we are because of the choices we make.

Knowing comes from doing. If you don't know love, live it with everything you have. If you don't know success, be it with all that you are. If you don't know sexy, do it from the inside out. We are not given the knowing, we are giving the opportunity to know which means it's time to try. If you don't like what you are getting you must change what you are doing to try to get a new result. It's that simple.

It's not what happens to you in life, but how you choose to deal with it. That choice is critical to what happens in your life. Start taking accountability for your own actions, beliefs, attitude, surroundings and results. The more love you have for yourself, the more you will attract those who also love themselves and you will be amazed at how quickly things and people who are not sexy, confident and positive will disappear.

Again, I remind you, that you attract that which you are, not that which you want. If you find yourself surrounded by difficult relationships, negativity, sadness, fear, lack of success, regret or anything else that you would prefer not to embrace, then it starts with you. Now more than ever, finding your sexy professional inner you is going to have a significant impact on your life and the people you attract.

Where do you spend your time, energy, emotion, passion, love and thoughts? Be careful of the things you want or chase, you may actually get them. We all want positive feedback-And many times, when people don't get the attention and feedback they desire, they go after negative attention or refocus their efforts on getting attention and feedback from the wrong people, which can further reduce your capacity to get what you want in life.

If you are still wondering how to become sexier, consider this. Most people are constantly thinking with their memory, not their imagination! Children use 98% of their imagination. As adults, people are so busy thinking about the past, that we do not use our imagination to re-invent the future. Adults spend 2% of time using their imagination to INVENT! That is the belief we need to grow…As adults-the plan to wait until later will prevent you from growing now.

If you are spending your time, thinking, dressing, living, money, training the same way you were 6 months ago, you are guaranteed to get the same results you have now, 6 months from now. If your network of people that you spend your time with is the same now as it was 6 months ago, 6 months from now you will be where you are today.

Change is not comfortable. You don't need to do it alone. It is however, required…at least to me it is.

We must become super competent at a niche group of things. To me, the following are my priorities for competency.

1. Continuous Change, Growth and Personal Development
2. Being a Mother-Consistency and Follow Through.
3. True Love, Partnership and Relationship Building
4. Financial Literacy, Making Money, Technology and Marketing.
5. Leadership and Strategy
6. Speaking, Presentation Skills and Overall Communication
7. Choosing Relationships. Significant Other, Friends, Family, Clients, Partners, Staff, Mentors, etc
8. Focus, Self Discipline, Commitment and Dedication
9. Say No to everything that does not fit in alignment.
10. Truly Enjoying Life and the World Around Me.

Practice on a daily basis-without changing or being judgmental about someone else. Concentrate on yourself. If possible, share your goal for becoming super competent with your spouse, business partners or mentors. Hopefully they have the ability to help hold you accountable. Turn your thoughts, emotions and energy internally.

The more you practice, the luckier you get. Most people don't have a plan, so what are they practicing. Success is the very thing that brings about failure, the fear of losing success is the very thing that keeps us from it. It's time to take action—so put on your sexy attitude and get to work.

My Sexy Quandary
By Maurice DiMino

As you can imagine, Hidi and I have a lot of conversations about 'What is Sexy?' A lot of conversations.

One morning when I was driving Hidi to work the topic came up again. And I remarked, sexy is related to one's occupation. Hidi asked me to elaborate.

For a few moments I stuttered and stammered and then blurted out: "Well take Chrissie Hynde for example." Hidi did not know who she is and so I had to explain that Hynde is the lead singer of the band The Pretenders. They had a couple of great hits in the 1980's: "Back on the Chain Gang"–"My City is Gone" to name a few.

Talking about Chrissie Hynde with Hidi made me wondered if she is sexy or is she sexy because of her profession: Lead Singer in a Popular Band.

I do have to admit that when I look at pictures of her or when I saw her on an episode of "Friends" when she played a character that was competing against Phoebe for the singing spot at the Central Perk coffee shop–I have to admit, I don't find her sexy. She's got a plain Pittsburg face with a boyish figure. Someone that I would not stop and tell you, "She's Sexy!"

But yet...yet...when I see or hear her sing–She's is so Sexy! When I saw her perform on Saturday Night Live in the late eighties, she was exuding so much sexiness. I could not take my eyes off of her. She was cat-like. That deep-throated voice! She's Sexy!

She is Sexy?

How could that be? A moment ago I said she's plain and boyish.

She and others always make me think: Is she sexy because of her occupation? You know how some people think that the lead singer of a hot band is sexy. Was I applying that to Hynde?

"The Strange, Mysterious and Sexy Case of Elaine Benes"
My inquiry of this matter continues with Elaine Benes. You remember who Elaine Benes is? She is the friend of Jerry Seinfeld on his TV show "Seinfeld" played by Julia Louis-Dreyfus.

When I first began watching the show in the early 90's–I did not think much of Elaine/Julia. Those big Goldilocks hair curls and that plain Brooklyn face.

But as the years went on and the show became a hit…My view of Elaine changed. As the years went on, Dreyfus got sexier and sexier. Was it because of that episode where she left an 'X-rated' voice message on Jerry's cell phone? Or was it because she took charge of J. Peterman's with an iron-fist? Or was it because of her profession…did it play into my concept of what is sexy:

Profession equals Sexy.

And it continues to today. Hidi and I enjoy watching HGTV's "Love It Or List It." One of the designers on the show is Hilary Farr. When I first began watching the show, I thought she was no big deal. She's got a plain Oxford face and a super standard body. Nothing to write or text home about.

I watched more and more episodes. I watched how she handled her contractors, problems that arouse and working with the disgruntled couples when those problems arouse. And in every situation she handled it with a steady resolve, with keen observations…Boring! I now think she is Sexy!

Watching Hilary move from one room to the next, explaining the renovations to the eager couple with that light English accent…Gets my blood boiling…She is Sexy!

Why?

Is it because she is Sexy? Or is it because of her occupation? Her profession?

For me, I believe it is because of her profession. For all of them.

Chrissie Hynde–Lead Singer, hot band.

Julia Louis Dreyfus–Lead character, top rated show.

Hilary Farr–Lead designer, top rated cable show.

I can share other examples of my Sexy Quandary. And I believe that all of them add up to: I think they are sexy because of their profession. It is my attraction to the level of achievement. It may be similar when a woman finds a successful man sexy. I guess it works the same for us males: Successful woman are Sexy. There I said it!

And now if you will excuse me, I am going to listen to "Brass in Pocket" as I watch Hilary convince a couple to Love It. Now, that's Sexy!

CONTRIBUTORS

Chapter 1

Happiness is Sexy!

By Ricky Powell

Ricky Powell is a Southern California native and grew up as a child actor working with some of Hollywood's biggest legends.

After graduating college, he began his second career behind the camera and has worked at NBC for the past 23 years where he continues to prep virtually every show that airs on the network as their Program Operations Manager.

Although Ricky has devoted his whole life to the entertainment industry, several years ago, he became passionate about the subject of happiness.

He is the founder of Lifelong Happiness.com, author of *Happiness Rocks: A Powerful Blueprint to Master the Art of Lifelong Happiness* and creator of Ricky Powell's Love Your Life System.

Aside from his job at NBC, Ricky is an author, speaker, coach and consultant for both individuals who want to experience happiness on a daily basis and for companies who want to improve their bottom line with employees who are engaged, productive and thrilled to be on the job.

LifelongHappiness.com

Ricky@LifelongHappiness

(805) 279-4222

Being Sexy

By Cinthia Gambino-Calderon

Cinthia is the face of Innergy Creative Enterprises which began its formation since late 2008. As a speaker Cinthia has been effectively facilitating and touching audiences for more than 15 years. Speaking on the themes of responsibility and action; Cinthia focuses her subject on reaching for goals with passionate determination and intelligent balance. Cinthia has also volunteered time to educate teens in high schools about drug abuse and displaying responsible behavior for a successful life. While working full time counseling and traveling the United States as a spokes model, Cinthia earned her B.S. degree in Human Development with an emphasis in Counseling and graduated *cum laude*. Further education includes life coaching certifications and a Masters of Science in Management.

Previous life experience has afforded her the joys and life lessons of being a child immigrant at age 10, teen mother at the age of 18, and cancer survivor at the age of 27; all of which have fine-tuned her belief that "there are lessons to be learned in everything and it's up to us what we do with them." Cinthia has developed a passion for experiencing life fully, and learning from each event for the purpose of living a life worth living. Cinthia's overall approach to life is filled with energy and that is what she brings to every interaction.

Innergy@CinthiaGambino.com
714-322-6169
Facebook: Cinthia Gambino-Calderon
YouTube: CinthiaTell

Did someone say "sexy"?
By Carrie Cray-Stewart
C.K. allowed her true passion to come alive, something deep within her whispered "this is your calling, your gift, don't run from your thoughts, run with them"…so she listened. This in turn lead to writing her first successful Bestselling "ROMANCE" novel…titled "Eye of the Storm" which is now in the process of being adapted to the BIG SCREEN!
www.ckgbooks.com
Twitter @ckgbooks
Facebook Fan page Love Story-Romance Novels by ckgbooks
Best Selling Romance Novelist- C.K. Gray "Eye of the Storm" and the sequel "After the Storm"

Love Yourself
By Ardiana Bani Cohn
Ardiana is a college instructor specializing in mathematics, science and psychology, a life coach, a speaker and an author. She wrote two books in the field of spirituality. Her books are a bit different and controversial from the rest of the spiritual books in the market. In her first book "Secret Beyond the Secret" Ardiana is introducing a new and original way of looking at destiny and the Law of Attraction. In her second book "The Twelve Laws of Living" Ardiana is using a theoretical away of laying out the logical and scientific facts that can conclude only one thing: The Existence of an Intelligent Mind.
www.knowthetruth.ca

Sexy is a State of Mind
By Elle Sompres
Elle Sompres began her career with 10 successful years in radio advertising–winning numerous awards. She became a National Sales Manager, was a career mentor for new reps & was nominated by her peers to head up the Leadership Board for 5 local radio stations. Elle has also been deeply immersed in personal & spiritual growth since the early 90s & came to realize she had the desire & skills to help others live a life they love & feel passionate about. So in 2004, she began working as a speaker/trainer for a national Personal Development company…learning everything she could about the speaking business. In 2008, she stepped out on her own to start a business called Inspired Success. She now delivers empowering speeches & also coaches people on how to work through limiting beliefs, heal emotional wounds that are keeping them stuck, reveal their own inner strength & take inspired action to create a life that truly rocks!

Elle lives in Santa Monica with her dog Ringo, attends Agape International Spiritual Center and enjoys painting, biking along the beach, reading, philanthropic work, live music & singing karaoke. She's truly a rockstar at heart.

www.inspired-success.com
elle@inspired-success.com
Office: 310-315-1842

Olympic Triathlon at Pacific Grove
By Nobuko Sezaki
Nobuko Sezaki shares her story of training and completing her first Olympic distance triathlon race. She has nothing to prove by completing the race. Most importantly, she treasures her experience of overcoming

her physical and mental barriers through testing her limits and growing from the inner strengths.

nobukosezaki@yahoo.com

Sexy Secret? Simple…Sacredness!

By Regiane Gorski

Regiane found Yoga in the 80's in Brazil and has practiced ever since. A previous ballet dancer she is a lover of movement and fluidity. She teaches vinyasa flow locally and around the World. She has lived in Australia, Hawaii and Los Angeles for the past 15 years, where she studied with a number of well known Yoga Teachers. Her interests also include metaphysics, human rights, women rights to name a few.

regianegorski.com

www.facebook.com/regiane.gorski

Chapter 2

Sexy From the Inside Out

By Sheryl Robinson

Sheryl is a part time freelance writer and a full time corporate director focusing on developing women into senior leadership positions. Sheryl lives with her two teenage sons in Monroe, New York and successfully manages a bi-coastal relationship with her hot California boyfriend.

sheryljr@hotmail.com

Time To Turn The Lights On

By Adryenn Ashley

Unabashed author Adryenn Ashley achieves the impossible: using laugh-out-loud humor she delivers essential information so effectively, you actually get it. An award winning, bestselling author of "Every Single Girl's Guide to Her Future Husband's Last Divorce", international speaker, and award winning filmmaker. Ashley's latest book, "Spotting

The Kooks" takes a hilarious look at the crazy world of dating and 19 most common kooks that waste your time and break your heart. Founder, Wow! Is Me.

http://wowisme.net

415-420-5627

Chapter 3
Transforming the Goddess...Unleashing Potential
By Rhonda Reed Clure

Rhonda Clure has a background in Clothing and Textiles with a Bachelors and Masters of Science Degree in Apparel Design from Kansas State University. She worked as a costumer in the film and television industry for 15 years. She started her own design company designing costumes and textile products for the film industry and the consumer market.

For the past 10 years she has been involved in the network marketing industry as a consultant for skincare, health and wellness products. One of her passions is to help people evaluate the safety of the products they use everyday and help them switch to non-toxic choices whenever possible. Rhonda is also a Distributor for Philip Martin Organics-US, a professional line of hair care and color, and a Director for TEAM Referral Network, helping to bring businesses in the community together so they can help each other by referring business to one another by building strong personal relationships. She is a member of the Conejo TEAM Partners Chapter.

Rhonda is a deeply passionate pole fitness instructor, and developed the "Unleash Your Inner Bombshell" program, helping women, especially those 30 and older learn a fun way to get fit and feel great in their own skin.

Rhonda is actively involved in the community and was the President of the Conejo Valley Kiwanis Club in 2009-2010, a service organization and also an active member of the <u>San Luis Obispo Women's Network</u> and a member of both Board of Directors.

805-498-4024

805-338-7431

<u>r_clure@yahoo.com</u>

<u>Simply Perfect Beauty</u>

<u>Simply Perfect Beauty on Facebook</u>

<u>Philip Martins Italian Organic Lifestyle</u>

Director TEAM Referral Network…Don't hire a sales TEAM…

Join one!

<u>GregClurePhotography.com</u>

ConejoKiwanis.org

"Kiwanis is a global organization of volunteers dedicated to changing the world one child and one community at a time."

My Evolution as a Woman of Substance

By Nancy Ferrari

Nancy Ferrari is the radio host of *The Nancy Ferrari Show* on W4CY Radio and iHeartRadio, and is also a life empowerment coach, inspirational speaker, author, contributing writer for numerous publications, sharing her messages of inspiration and living an empowered life. Nancy is also a co-author of *Contagious Optimism* and the awarding-winning and best-seller, *Selling With Synchronicity*.

Nancy is also the founder and CEO of Nancy Ferrari Media & Mentoring, providing media and mentoring programs to attain personal and professional success, utilizing her signature coaching programs based on the principles within her book *Discover the Essence of You*.

<u>www.nancyferrari.com</u>

<u>nancy@nancyferrari.com</u>

Sizzzlin' Sexy at Sixty
By Suzy Manning
Suzy Manning is the CEO of Suzy Manning, "helping women gain purpose, empowerment, and inner peace at midlife". She is an insightful mentor, an inspirational speaker, thought-provoking author, and savvy radio show host. Her expertise is helping female business owners and entrepreneurs discover their life purpose so they can live with clarity and passion. Suzy loves dance, cycling and juicing, being a grandmother, spending time in nature, and exploring new opportunities in life with her husband.

www.suzymanning.com

suzy@suzymanning.com

Sprinting to Sixty
By Patricia Karen Gagic
Patricia Gagic is an International Contemporary Artist, Photographer, Author of "Karmic Alibi"and a Business Mentor/Coach/Strategist and Consultant living in Canada. Ambassador to Ambassadors for World Peace, Global Enrichment Foundation,Friends to Mankind, Somaly Mam Foundation and Project Cambodia in Angkor Wat. Certified in Applied Mindfulness and Mindfulness Without Borders from the University of Toronto and Certified Feng Shui level II Consultant and Reiki Master. Nominated for Hamilton Woman of the Year Award, YMCA Peace Medal, YWCA Lifetime Achievement Award and recipient of First Annual Award of Excellence from the Toronto Women's Expo.Patricia mentored with Dragan Dragic in France and exhibits in Europe, North America and Korea. Represented by Peak Gallery Toronto, Gallery on the Bay Hamilton and BB International Fine Arts in Caslano, Switzerland.

www.inspiredtoberewired.com

patgagic@gmail.com

Sexy, No Matter the Time and Life Circumstances
By Carol Wagner
Carol Wagner, MS, is the CEO of a company which provides education on geriatric subjects such as Challenges of Adapting to Long Term Care; Grief, Death and Dying; Alzheimer's: A Challenge for Care, Sexuality and the Aged and many more subjects that may be viewed at www. bestsourcelc.com.

Chapter 4
The Scars of Time Are Just Lines
By Amy Regenstreif
Amy Regenstreif LTCP/CLTC has been a patient advocate for thousands in her 12 years of battling this disease.

She also has an insurance practice with New York Life Insurance Company since 2003. Her specialties are life insurance, annuities, and long term care insurance.

Amy has twin daughters 23 years old. They are out of college and working! :)

Amy jokes around a lot…she says she has no "spare time". She tries to do everything all of the time!

VisionBoardForaCure.com

(818) 406 9228

It's an everyday Deal!
By Mayra Abruzzo.
Mayra C. Aburto is a writer/illustrator living in California with her husband, sons, and her dog Biscuit. She was diagnosed with cancer in 2010. While recovering, she's been focusing on enjoying life to the fullest one day at a time, leading her to write a book to help other patients do the same.

Chapter 5

Relaxing Into My Sexy

By Amy Cheryl

Amy Cheryl is the founder of "Smart, Sexy and Spiritual," inspiring, educating, and empowering women to heal their shame and liberate their sexy selves to become the best version of themselves in business and beyond!

After losing over 80 pounds as a teenager, Amy knew she wanted to help inspire others. Being in the fitness industry for over 20 years, her heart's calling and life purpose work propelled Amy down a deep spiritual and healing journey, into becoming a Healing Arts Therapist. Since then, she has been the Spokesperson and Speaker for a 7-figure Business Coaching Company, sharing stages with Women Leaders including Marianne Williamson. Amy currently mentors women on "The Art of The Power Principles of The Feminine" through her "S.H.I.N.E." System in bringing their sexy back so they can have the business they desire and the life they deserve.

She has been published in several national magazines including SHAPE and SELF, invited to speaking engagements in Dubai and all over the U.S., and interviewed on several radio shows. Originally from New York, Amy currently resides in sunny Los Angeles.

To book Amy for speaking engagements or coaching, check out her website, and remember to get your FREE gift at www.amycheryl.com/freegift

Contact Info: #310.867.3766

Email: begroundedandsoar@gmail.com

What really Matters

By Jack M. Zufelt

He has discovered something that is being called a "breakthrough" and a "wake up call" in the world of success and personal development. He overcame huge obstacles and disadvantages to become a very successful man with a vast amount of experience in many different arenas. Jack is the Author of the #1 bestselling book, The DNA of Success, which is now in 15 languages.

Jack was awarded the Presidential Medal of Merit by a President of the United States. He was honored by the United States Senate for teaching Americans how to achieve better results in their personal lives and careers.

He has been interviewed on over 2,000 radio and TV talk shows including The TODAY SHOW. PBS aired a special on Jack and his concepts that was sent via satellite to 127 countries.

"Mentor to Millions" Author of the #1 Best Selling Book "The DNA of Success" And several best-selling audio programs. Sold in 50 countries

www.jackzufeltspeaks.com

www.DNAofSuccess.com

FaceBook: www.facebook.com/jackzufeltfan

Finding Sexiness No Matter What

By Janice Ogata

Janice Ogata is the immediate past President of Warner Bros. Toastmasters In 2013-2014 she will be an Area Governor in the Toastmaster organization. She is the founder of "The Pasadena Crochet Meet Up" and a member of 7 different knitting and crocheting groups. She enjoys knitting for charity and lives in Southern California with her roommate and a cat named Grey Kitty. She is also a blogger for Red Heart Yarns and can be reached via email for interviews and public speaking engagements.

janiceogata@gmail.com

Chapter 6

Why don't men cover their faces?

By Hind Aleryani

She is a Yemeni activist and working as a journalist at NOW. She contributed significantly to the famous #ShameOnReuters campaign… and several campaigns against the drug Khat

https://twitter.com/HindAleryani

http://doryaleryani.blogspot.com

Levi's Cowboy boots and Tee shirts

By Kathleen DePuydt

Kathleen (Kat) DePuydt is a short story author and novelist. Her short story "It is Lovely, No?" was published in the anthology 95% Naked, Fictions and Nonfictions, and "Of Mice and Me" published in Tiny Lights: A Journal of Personal Narrative. Currently, she is a member of the writing group Right Night to Write with Christine Walker. Originally from Montana, she now lives in Santa Rosa, California with her partner, Terry, and two cats, Fuzzy and Snoopy.

You can contact her at kdepuydt@earthlink.net

'Sexy with No Boundaries'—
In the eyes of an American-Muslim Woman

By Sarah Khan

Public Speaker

http://www.ksarahsarah.org

www.ksarahsarah.org

Chapter 7

Recipe for Sexy

By Helen Woo

Helen Woo is host of the weekly radio talk show *"Self Aid Success Stories"* http://toginet.com/shows/SelfAidSuccessStories. She inspires listeners to laugh and reminds them that all challenges can be conquered, starting with *"Self-Aid"* (self-help). Helen's theme song for her show is *"I Will Survive"* by Gloria Gaynor. This is a personal proclamation. Inspirational and empowering stories of triumph over life's challenges take over the airwaves during this hour. Helen would love to have you share your story, too!

Helen Woo has recently been published in Wake Up Women's latest book "Be You-Spread Your Wings and Fly" with her story, "I am Flying High and I am Here to Flourish".

Watch for her upcoming book: *"Self-Aid–Inspirations to Turn Struggles to Success"*, a book on Helen's thoughts and inspirations that helped her to fight her many challenges throughout her life.

Her second book will follow: *"Self-Aid Success Stories"* which will include a collection of triumphant stories from inspirational leaders of how they conquered their challenges.

Helen's third book *"Principles of Self-Aid"* is in the making as well.

Besides writing, Helen also enjoys public speaking and media. She has a big YouTube presence, and she is creating programs that will support others in breaking free from situations that keep them from living their best lives.

www.SelfAidSuccessStories.com

www.TheHelenWoo.com

HelenWoo@SelfAidSuccessStories.com

Twitter: @SelfAidSuccess

Nothing Feels Sexier Than Your Own Firm & Fit Body
By Brian Kelly
Brian Kelly is a P90X Certified Professional and founder of Global Fitness Club, an internet-based venue that provides live online workouts completely free of charge.

His mission is not just to end the trend of obesity, but also to end the trend of what he calls "F.D.D.", or, Fitness Deficite Disorder-a condition often found in busy business professionals, moms, and students.

Brian founded Global Fitness Club at the age of 48 after receiving alarming results from a routine health screen. From that moment, he vowed to commit to his own health and fitness, and is now sharing his mission with everyone who has the desire to get and/or stay fit.

GlobalFitnessClub.com
brian@brianckelly.com

Chapter 8

Living from the inside out
By Dina Blas
Dina Blas is a Confidence Coach and Mentor, Inspirational and Motivational Speaker, Expert Interviewer and Author. She founded Your Voice Your Life as a way to help women discover their potential, know their possibilities, set their goals, make decisions and take powerful action steps so that they can live their lives with passion.

After losing her father at the age of 12, overcoming a sheltered and restrictive upbringing in the Middle East, and then finally "coming out" at the age of 25, Dina uncovered a powerful and dynamic voice within her that needed to be shared. She believes that women need an outlet to discover their true identity (their "voice") and spark their existence (their "life"). As a coach and mentor, she provides a safe and inviting environment for women to discover themselves again and all the possibilities that still await them.

"In order to change the world, we must start with ourselves and then pass it forward." ~Coach Dina Blas

www.DinaBlas.com

Dina@DinaBlas.com

Phone: (707) 902-3462

Facebook: www.facebook.com/YourVoiceYourLife

Twitter: Coach_DinaBlas

How do you feel sexy?

By Svetlana V. Ray

Born and raised in the capital of a small exotic European country–Bulgaria–Svetlana has been passionate to learn and share her learning with others. A near-death experience early in her life determined her direction for expansion of her worldly views. Graduated from high school with a Gold medal, moved straight to University, Svetlana completed three majors in 6 years–M.Sc. in Electronics and Automations, Journalism and Management and Marketing. Few years later, Svetlana immigrates to the United States of America.

After her initial struggles, she attends American Colleges studying Finance, Accounting, Real Estate, and finally–her destiny takes her to Hypnosis Motivational Institute where she graduates with Honors and Academic Awards. Now, in her therapy practice, Svetlana helps others to achieve personal goals and make desired changes in their lives. Svetlana believes that inner peace is the ultimate aspiration for all human beings and when achieved by many–the world will become a better place for all.

Svetlana V. Ray, C.Ht

The Power of One Reflective Therapy

Transformational Body Shaping Program

Phone: 818-371-7693

www.SvetlanaRay.com

Chapter 9
Professional and Sexy by Design within your Mind
By Jennifer Bagley

Jennifer Bagley is one of the most in-demand Sales Supply Chain, Personal Development and Business Marketing Strategists. She is known for her engaging and entertaining style, as well as, her mastery level knowledge of the Sales Supply Chain-including Technology, Strategy, Behavior and Collaborative Marketing Strategies.

Jennifer Bagley is the Founder of DNet a Digital Network, co-founder of Sales Supply Chain Consulting, the Founder of CI Web Group, a Digital Marketing Company and is the Vice President of Strategy for Mothernode CRM and ERP. In today's ultra-competitive world, getting superior results faster is absolutely critical to success! So many want it! However, this hectic speed of life makes it easy to become side-tracked by things that steal priority and make us less effective. People are hungry for ways to get ahead, to win, to accelerate results both personally and professionally. Jennifer will address this desire.

www.JenniferBagley.com
www.DNetTV.com
www.SalesSupplyChain.com
www.CIWebGroup.com
Phone: 972-342-5933

My Sexy Quandary
By Maurice DiMino

Imagine taking the number one fear, Public Speaking, and making it your number one asset?

Maurice DiMino does just that. He trains executives and entrepreneurs how to use their presentations as an income generating tool for their product, service or charity. He has developed an easy to use template so that you can create raving fans. Go from zero to hero with Confidence, Character and Charisma.

Maurice is the author of the book "The Art of Public Speaking". He has given over 2,000 paid presentations, seven years on the speaking circuit and has developed battle tested techniques.

In 2004, Los Angeles Toastmasters voted him "Best Speaker".

The TED Organization recognized him as an outstanding speaker and in April 2013 he became a TEDx speaker at San Diego State University.

He has taken his book, his years of experience of being a corporate speaker and made it into a boot camp..."Discover Your Million Dollar Message". At his Intensive—you will create a Profitable, Passionate and Powerful presentation for your product, service or charity.

Visit his website and sign-up for a free thirty minute consultation!

Maurice DiMino

The Million Dollar Message Expert

Maurice@MauriceDiMino.com

www.MauriceDiMino.com

POSTSCRIPT

I have a dream that one day every man and woman will look into their mirror and fall in love with what they see.

I have a dream that one day we are judged by the content of our inner beauty, and not the superficial outer appearances.

I have a dream that one day we have such a peace within ourselves that no one can interfere with our inner mind.

I have a dream that this "one day" is approaching us sooner than anybody thinks. Now is the time to speak for love, generosity, kindness, integrity and peace. And I say to you my friends, let my dream be contagious. Let this message spread to your friends, your family, your colleagues, your neighbors…

If you admit that this book has widened your view on what sexy is about nowadays, and it helps you to feel better about who you are, please either pass the book on to those you might think can be benefit from it; or recommend it to your friends and family. I do believe some people have to be the change-makers, and I hope this book can be part of that much-needed wave of change. And together, we can make a better world. Somewhere in my mind, lives the Dalai Lama's wisdom, "If you think you are too small to make a difference, try sleeping with a mosquito."

This book is the first one of the whole series. It will be followed by "Love with No Boundaries", "Dream with No Boundaries" and "Success with No Boundaries"…It's never too early to contribute your real life story to my books. Let's join forces to mark the movement!

You can e-mail your story to hidi@hidilee.com, with the subject title as to fit into which one of my book. Please do not forget to include the title of your story, your short bio and your website or contact info. This is my way of sharing the spotlight. People also like to ask me how many words I am looking for, I will say from at least one page to maximum 5 pages. I believe that the power of content doesn't rely on the length of the story.

I remember I went to see the International Speech Contest from Toastmasters once. The winner gave a speech of 5-7 minutes and he made the whole audiences cry (both men and women)! That was the power of your story! I don't mean that you have to make the readers cry, but, you know what I mean.

If your story is chosen to be published, you will get my autographed copy as a thank you gift from me. On top of that, anything I do in marketing and promotion, you will instantly become part of the promotion because you are the co-author of the book.

I like what Lady Gaga said in one of her concert, "I want you to walk out of here tonight not loving me more, but loving yourselves more." I am going to take her as my inspiration—I want you to finish reading this book not loving me more, but loving yourselves more. Know that YOU are beautiful and sexy in your own way. And if you feel so, please pass the book on so others can benefit from it too. Thank you!

For more about me, and what I do, please visit www.HidiLee.com or connect with me at Hidi@HidiLee.com

Sincerely,

Hidi Lee

OTHER PRODUCTS BY HIDI LEE

Her book "Almost Naked–Lingerie, Secret of the Guilty Pleasure"
A book combines the history, psychology and sociology of lingerie. The diversities of different real life stories supported her vision how lingerie plays an important part in relationship. Discover how lingerie can fire-up your relationship—whether it is between you and your partner; or you with yourself.
$16

The Naked Truth–Live Workshop
An event that redefines sensuality and breaks through false body perceptions
Join Hidi Lee and Maureen Benoit to a life changing event from self discovery and inspiration and confirmation to a sensual, successful and positive future.
$47

To Be Your Own Image Consultant–4 Audio CD set
Discover Your Own Fashion DNA
Discover Your Own Fashion DNA
Discovering your own personality
Finding your skin tone and body shape
Learn the power of visual illusion
Develop a Fashion Sense
Get the insider tips to maximize your budget
$127

To Be Your Own Image Consultant–
4 consecutive Live Tele-webinars
Discover Your Own Fashion DNA
Discovering your own personality
Finding your skin tone and body shape
Learn the power of visual illusion
Develop a Fashion Sense
Get the insider tips to maximize your budget
(Details upon request)

To Be Your Own Image Consultant–Live Intensive
Discover Your Own Fashion DNA
Small group to work closely with The Image
Expert to discover everything you need to find
your own personal style from the inside out
$347

The Fashion Confession–Live Seminar
The Truth of the Fashion World
(For today's college and high school students)

Find out from an array of different experts from the fashion industry to have a reality check to the fashion position that you have been dreaming of. Get a clear picture and jump leap ahead of all those. (Details upon request)

The Image Expert
Life 1 on 1 Coaching program
Go one on one with The Image Expert to work on:
Creating your personal style
Developing your sense of fashion
Planning your wardrobe budget
Organizing your fashion closet
(Details upon request)

Please visit her fashion and lingerie blog www.Lingerissimi.com–An intellectual dimension within the sensual world of lingerie

Don't forget to visit her website HidiLee.com
Hidi Lee is available for keynotes, workshops, breakout sessions, panel discussion and personal coaching or styling. From personal assistant, to college to corporate—bring in Hidi Lee for a fun, interactive and informative session

For products or to book Hidi Lee–
Please connect through e-mail: Hidi@HidiLee.com

ABOUT THE AUTHOR

Having worked as a lingerie designer for the past 24 years, Hidi had worked with all different sizes and shapes of women in her fitting room. From Hong Kong, to Italy, to Canada, to United States, Hidi believes that no matter where she works, she faces the same kind of woman, the one that is confused and insecure in her own body.

Having walked down that path herself, she realized that it is a major block to any kind of success—relationship, personal development, social acceptance and career growth. She decided to create a social movement–a movement that will awake every single individual to fall in love with themselves; starting from the most inner depth of her body, her soul and her mind.

Through her lingerie, books, workshops and speeches, she empowers women to redefine their inner beauty and achieve a body that every woman wants to have and every man wants his woman to have. Her ultimate goal is to turn the once confused and insecure woman into a confident, sexy and successful woman.

BOOK REVIEW

International lingerie fashion designer Hidi Lee, author of "Almost Naked", once again brings truth to life in her newest book <u>Sexy with no Boundaries</u>. Women all over the world have made great strides toward equal humanity over the last century yet as Hidi Lee points out, many still feel inferior. Always the trailblazer, Hidi creates a veritable pathway to a new understanding and a recipe for success regardless of a woman's age, color, creed, disability, education, illness, nationality, socioeconomic group, or body image.

We are all special—we are all sexy—and these beautifully written pages describe sexy in a very different light than the traditional. As a Film Producer, I frequently see women objectified by others but also by themselves. It is with the greatest of pleasure that I encourage you to view these issues through Hidi's eyes. I promise-you will uncover unseen beauty in all its forms.

—**Mary Cimiluca**, Producer, Noetic Films, Inc.,
Beverly Hills, California

"The beauty of Hidi's book, and the reason anyone and everyone should pick it up to read it, is in the diversity of the voices, viewpoints and stories written by Hidi and her contributors.

As a young person about to enter the work force, I particularly enjoyed Hidi and the other authors' advice and thoughts on dressing for work, maintaining personal confidence and expressing oneself. Readers who enjoy self-reflection and improvement will love this book and find it enlightening and informative. I highly recommend Hidi's book-Sexy with no Boundaries!"

—**Amanda T.**, Esq.

"Hidi Lee captures the essence of "Sexy" in her new book—Sexy with No Boundaries. It is an immensely pleasurable read because of her unique perspective on a subject that is so personal to all of us. Not only has Hidi provided her own perspective on Sexy throughout the book, but she also collected stories about SEXY from an eclectic group of accomplished people that each provide their unique perspective.

These stories run the gamut from dealing with adversity, challenging social taboos, to finding the inner definition of Sexy. The stories are all very personal and eye-opening. The contributor's stories make you feel like you are talking to friends with a glass of wine and hearing them share something very interesting and intensely personal. The result is a better understanding of Sexy and how we all can take steps to remove the boundaries to our personal definition of "Sexy"."

—**Rick Chandler**, Director of Marketing Kretek International

CPSIA information can be obtained at www.ICGtesting.com
Printed in the USA
BVOW07s1014260614

357468BV00004B/96/P